The Diplomacy of Prudence
Canada and Israel, 1948–1958

The Diplomacy of Prudence is an analysis of Canadian foreign policy during the first decade of Israeli independence. Zachariah Kay argues that the Canadian government was cautious in its support of Israel, attempting to maintain a balanced position between the warring Arab and Israeli sides.

Using a case study approach, Kay explores Canada's response to key issues such as the recognition of the new state of Israel, the status of Jerusalem, the Palestinian refugee problem, arms sales to Israel, particularly the sale of F-86s in 1956, and the Suez war. He also provides a thorough account of domestic politics in Canada that influenced foreign policy and the effectiveness of pro-Israeli lobby groups in influencing policy decisions. Kay concludes that although Canada was a major middle power in terms of its policy towards Israel, the government tended to defer to the policy positions of greater powers, such as the United States and Britain, but maintained an independent mediatory role that was instrumental in quelling a prospective global conflagration, as witnessed during the Sinai-Suez crisis and its aftermath.

The Diplomacy of Prudence brings new insights to the study of Canadian foreign policy during Canada's coming of age as an international force.

ZACHARIAH KAY was an elected member of the Canadian Political Science Executive and is an executive member of the Israel Association for Canadian Studies.

The Diplomacy of Prudence

Canada and Israel, 1948–1958

ZACHARIAH KAY

McGill-Queen's University Press
Montreal & Kingston • London • Buffalo

© McGill-Queen's University Press 1996
ISBN 0-7735-1435-X

Legal deposit fourth quarter 1996
Bibliothèque nationale du Québec

Printed in the United States on acid-free paper

Canadian Cataloguing in Publication Data

Kay, Zachariah
    The diplomacy of prudence: Canada
    and Israel, 1948–1958

    Includes bibliographical references and index.
    ISBN 0-7735-1435-X

    1. Canada – Foreign relations – Israel.
    2. Israel – Foreign relations – Canada.
    3. Canada – Foreign relations – 1945– I. Title.

    FC251.I7K39 1997   327.7105694   c96-990013-9
    F1029.5.I7K39 1997

To the Cherished Memory of
My Mother Rose

Contents

Note on Sources

Primary sources for this work included official publications from Canadian and Israeli government departments as well as the files of the National Archives of Canada (NA) and the Israel State Archives (ISA). Secondary sources are cited only in the endnotes. The reader should note that the Pearson papers contain many documents that originally appeared in the files of the Department of External Affairs and that in these cases reference has generally been to the DEH files.

Many documents in the Israel State Archives series Documents on the Foreign Policy of Israel (DFPI) are in English, some are in French, and quite a number are in Hebrew. The relevant texts have been translated into English.

Canada, Ottawa. House of Commons, *Debates*, 1949–58
  Senate, *Debates*, 1948–58
  Department of External Affairs
    publications, statements and speeches
    Privy Council files, 1947–58
  House of Commons: Standing Committee on External Affairs
  Minutes
  National Archives of Canada
    files of the Department of External Affairs RG 25 series
    Privy Council files from 1947, RG 2 series
    Papers of E.L.M. Burns, MG 31
    John G. Diefenbaker, MG 26

Lester B. Pearson, MG 26
Louis S. St Laurent, MG 26
Israel, Sdeh Boker. Ben Gurion Archives, diaries, 1948–58
  Israel State Archives: Foreign Office Files: *Documents on the
  Foreign Policy of Israel*, vols. 1–7, 1948–52 (English and Hebrew)
  and Companion vols., 1948–52 (English)

Preface

This book is a sequel to my previous study on the subject, *Canada and Palestine: The Politics of Non-Commitment* (Jerusalem: Israel Universities Press, 1978). It is an account of Canada's diplomatic relations with Israel based upon primary sources from the national archives of both countries. Once all documents became available for perusal, the work was carried out in Jerusalem and Ottawa.

The late Michael Comay, who served as the first head of the (British) Commonwealth division in Israel's Foreign Ministry and subsequently its first ambassador to Canada during the decade under study was to have collaborated in this work. Tragically, he succumbed to cancer during the initial stage of the study. His centrality in the first decade is axiomatic and his sagacity was sorely missed. His contribution would undoubtedly have enhanced the end product.

While the work was in progress, I presented four papers which were to eventually appear as chapters in the book. The presentations were made at the conferences of the Australian and New Zealand Association of Canadian Studies in Armadale, New South Wales, July 1990; the Association of Canadian Studies of the United States, Boston, November 1991; the Southwest Association of Canadian Studies, Lafayette, Louisiana, February 1993; and finally the Western Social Science Association, Oakland, California, April 1995.

This study was made possible through a major grant from the Samuel and Sadye Bronfman Family Foundation enabling its inauguration and early sustenance. Several other grants facilitated its continuation which included the Programme in Canadian Studies –

now a Centre – of the Hebrew University of Jerusalem; the Jewish Foundation of Manitoba; the late Arye Dulzin, chair of the Jewish Agency from the Chair's research fund; the Social Sciences and Humanities Research Council of Canada; and the Israel Association for Canadian studies for research, travel and publication grants. My sincere thanks for their vital assistance.

Thanks are also due to Avraham Avi-Hai, a former member of the Jewish Agency executive for his early assistance and encouragement; to David Smith and other members of the National Archives of Canada staff, with a very special thanks to Ian McClymont of the Manuscripts Division; the personnel of External Affairs Historical Division, library and the embassy staff in Tel Aviv; and to the staff of the Israel State Archives, with special thanks to Yehoshua Freundlich.

I would also like to express my appreciation to the following who read and commented on segments of the draft manuscript: Michael Brecher, McGill political science professor; the late Avraham Harman, long-time president and chancellor of the Hebrew University of Jerusalem; Geoffrey Wigoder, editor-in-chief of Encyclopaedia Judaica; Yosef Yaacov, retired Israeli diplomat, and the McGill-Queen's editors.

Finally, what follows is my sole responsibility.

Introduction

Canada's development from colony to Dominion and quasi-sovereignty by the conclusion of the Second World War was accompanied by gradual evolution to measured self-reliant decision making in foreign policy. From Confederation until 1946, almost eight full decades, there was no separate External Affairs minister: from the department's founding in 1909 the prime minister always retained the portfolio. Between 1946 and 1948 the new, separate minister – and presumed successor to the long-time Liberal prime minister – remained very much under Mackenzie King's sway. Nonetheless External Affairs personnel were already asserting themselves and becoming quite active in the post-war international arenas. By then Canada had emerged as a major middle power due to its physical size, considerable industrial growth, and wartime contribution to the Allied effort. As a geographic titan, it was strategically interposed between the two superpowers: however, for economic, historical, ideological, political and social reasons, it was strongly allied to the United States.

All such factors are reasons for a cautious approach to international relations. Canada's only palpable reason to engage in commitments beyond her alliances with the u.s. and Britain was to establish an international organization dedicated to peace and security.

For pragmatic reasons, the Holy Land was too remote to be a logical place to which to make foreign policy commitments. The religious factors, while not necessarily based on Hebrew messianism, Koranic scriptures, or papal precepts on Protestant fundamentalism, were not primary considerations in decision making. Indeed, Canada followed a policy of noncommitment as far as Palestine was concerned until Jewish sovereignty was restored there in 1948. That policy was predicated on the views of a very cautious and reluctant prime minister whose legacy the succeeding government somewhat modified for the post-1948 decade. Hence a natural transition from noncommitment to caution or weighty prudence that preceded Canada's *de facto* recognition of Israel was followed by another delay in *de jure* recognition which came simultaneously with United Nations membership for the Jewish state. It was indicative of what was to follow.

This study is based on the cases and issues which dominated the military and political relationship between Israel and Canada in Israel's first decade. The status of Jerusalem, a delicate issue, ordained a particularly cautious approach for a country headed by a Roman Catholic. Still Canada demurred from the Vatican's demands for the full internationalization of the city and its environs. Concern for the Palestinian refugee manifested itself in material support and was a factor in Canada's Middle Eastern concern for decades in spite of the commonly held perception of Canada's pro-Israel stance.

The most pronounced manifestation of prudent diplomacy were armaments in general and the struggle over the Sabre jets sale in particular. Added to that were the predilections and proclivities of Ottawa's bureaucrats. The chapters dealing with those matters bring into sharper focus the theme of this study.

The trauma of the Sinai-Suez operation in the autumn of 1956 was the primary factor which raised Canadian involvement in the Arab-Israel conflict to an apex from which it was to recede in subsequent decades. Yet the government – particularly its External Affairs minister and his close advisors, confirmed Canada as a major middle power with a proper sense of timing combined with circumspection and a palatable plan to quell a prospective global conflagration. The balance in the Canadian-Israeli relationship was maintained and continued even with the change in the federal government toward the first decade's conclusion.

The first decade of Canada-Israeli relations is a story of a major middle power and its relationship with a new state that had already acquired a reputation as a regional power. In a world galvanized into bi-polarity with the Cold War, this decade appears to have been one of the chilliest periods.

The Diplomacy of Prudence

1 From Recognition to Full Diplomacy

More than seven months were to pass after the proclamation of the State of Israel on the Sabbath eve of 14 May 1948 before the Canadian government granted *de facto* recognition. During that period Canada reached a watershed in the course of its foreign policy in general and on the Middle East in particular. The significance lies in the changes in leadership at the apex of the Canadian federal polity. A civil servant had risen through the ranks to become External Affairs minister with a substantial control of his portfolio, unimpeded by a prime minister chary – as his predecessor – about international involvements.

Secretary of State for External Affairs, Louis Stephen St Laurent, had been elected Liberal Party leader at the August 1948 convention in Ottawa and became prime minister on 15 November. He had finally succeeded William Lyon Mackenzie King who by then had established an apparently insurmountable record as the longest-serving prime minister in the British Empire and Commonwealth. St Laurent's successor in External Affairs and long-time civil servant Lester Bowles "Mike" Pearson had played a key role in the establishment of the United Nations Special Committee on Palestine (UNSCOP) and in husbanding its majority recommendation on the partition of Palestine into separate Arab and Jewish states in the General Assembly the previous year.[1] That had significantly enhanced his diplomatic standing in world forums. Pearson was sworn in on 10 September 1948, and entered the House of Commons after winning a by-election on 25 October.

Pearson's move from deputy minister – formally known as under-secretary – to major political decision maker in the era of Liberal parliamentary hegemony also enhanced his position in the house and on the hustings. It enabled him to further pursue his career as a seeker of *détente* in interstate relations.[2] As a consequence of his subsequent efforts, particularly during the Sinai-Suez crisis and in the creation of the United Nations Emergency Force (UNEF), he won the international acclaim that culminated in the Nobel Peace Prize at the end of 1957, almost at the conclusion of the decade in which he was the dominant figure in laying the foundation for prudential Canadian-Israeli relations in the far more pacific decade which followed. The period has been described as "The Emergence of Liberal International-ism, 1947–1957."[3]

Paradoxically, the decade began with the conclusion in power of the self-effacing and British-oriented William Lyon Mackenzie King. Indeed, King's attitudes had become anachronistic in the post-war world in which Canada had emerged as a major middle power. More-over, as under-secretary, Pearson was too politically active for the likes of Mackenzie King in his role at the United Nations and had caused a cabinet crisis over the partition plan. In fact, he "had stuck out his neck."[4] In his new ministerial capacity and with a firm grip on the External Affairs portfolio, "sticking (his) neck out" as a cabinet member and trusted successor to the new prime minister would cer-tainly be in contrast to Pearson's previous status. The decade proved sufficiently rewarding for him on the national political stage as well: he was to succeed St Laurent as party leader and prime minister half way through the second decade of Canadian-Israeli relations.

Canada's midwifery role at the conception and birth of the UN General Assembly's partition plan has been well recorded.[5] Yet Canadian policy makers were chagrined by the subsequent behaviour of the two main anglophone powers. Pearson's predecessor as under-secretary and then High Commissioner in London, Norman Robert-son, was annoyed with the British government. In a communication to Pearson he stated that we "may soon see the United Kingdom moving out of its exasperatingly negative role and taking its share of responsibility in the task of conciliation."[6] That of course was not to be. In a subsequent communication to Robertson in the wake of Is-rael's declaration of independence, Pearson stated: "So far as I am con-cerned, my own impatience with the attitude and policy of the United Kingdom and the United States toward Palestine has not been dimin-ished by the developments of the last week. The legal argument of the United Kingdom that there is no difference between Arabs invading Palestine and Jews who may be attempting to set up a state within a United Nations resolution, does not impress me very favourably, though no doubt it is explained by strategy and oil. On the other hand, the United States revolving-door policy, each push determined to a large extent by domestic political considerations and culminating in the sorry recognition [of Israel] episode of last Saturday, inspires no confidence and warrants little support."[7]

While Pearson might have been irked by United States President Harry Truman's rapid grant of *de facto* recognition of Israel's statehood, he could well have anticipated that the renascent Jewish state would seek Canada's recognition, particularly in the light of its role at the United Nations. On 7 June Michael Saul Comay, head of the fledgling Israel Foreign Ministry's British Commonwealth division, met with George Ignatieff, who was then with the Canadian delegation at the United Nations. General A.G.L. McNaughton, who headed the Canadian delegation, was very much of the Mackenzie King mind insofar as the prime minister desired a non-activist role for Canada. The same could be said of Justice Minister J.L. Ilsley, who had cast Canada's vote for partition on 29 November 1947. Ignatieff, on the other hand, was very much a "Pearsonian" who felt the Jews should have some territorial guarantee. He had established a rapport with Israelis Eliahu Elath (né Epstein), Abba Eban, and foreign minister Moshe Sharett (né Shertok), who tried to make the best of the partition plan. Ignatieff was reporting directly to Pearson[8] and suggested that Comay go to Ottawa to present Israel's case for recognition, which he did on 21 June.[9] Comay argued that there was a legal and moral obligation for recognition which flowed form the partition resolution of 29 November 1947. Noting Canada's middle power status and that it was "unencumbered by any special status in the Palestine issue," Comay cited the country's membership in the UN Security Council. Since the partition resolution contemplated the new state's admission to the United Nations, a Security Council recommendation was a prerequisite, making Canada's recognition indispensable. Aware of British policy and its impact on the Mackenzie King government, Comay felt assured that the United Kingdom would follow the anticipated Canadian "lead in due course."[10]

Comay's brief was followed with additional correspondence seeking to ascertain the Canadian government's attitude on Israel's United Nations membership.[11] Pearson was well aware that there should be some time lag between Canadian and British recognition of Israel. Indeed, the External Affairs minister was ahead of cabinet and even his staff on the recognition question as he related it to Israel's Foreign Minister Moshe Sharett at the November General Assembly sessions in Paris: "Pearson even confessed that he, personally, was in favour of recognition, but that the majority of the cabinet wishes to avoid a clash with Britain."[12]

In the conversation with Sharett, Pearson advised Israel not to become "so dazzled by her might that she attempt to seize the remainder of western Palestine by force." He further suggested that a compromise had to be found with Israel's demand for the Negev region, which was opposed by the British. As for the current United Nations session, Pearson concluded that "(1) there was no need to finalize the borders during this session; (2) the [Palestine] Conciliation Commission should be a Good Offices Committee;[13] (3) Israel should be admitted to the United Nations during this session, so that she might enjoy equal status with the Arabs before the Commission."[14]

Pearson's conclusions still had to be confirmed by his own government and even bureaucrats where the British impact was still intact. External Affairs' Elizabeth MacCallum noted in a memorandum to the acting minister that "Canada would be reluctant to become the state casting the deciding vote," while Escott Reid, her External Affairs colleague, noted for Pearson that the admission issue should be distinct from recognition.[15] Deep Israeli disappointment was communicated to Pearson on 18 December, with Comay claiming that Canada was one of those responsible for the rejection of Israel's application.[16]

Eliahu Elath, Israel's representative and subsequently its first ambassador to the United States, noted, "Vacillating Canada followed France under British pressure" on the United Nations membership issue.[17] According to Israel's United Nation's representative Abba Eban, 'Pearson was favourably disposed, but unsure as to the appropriate timing."[18] To some it was clear the External Affairs minister was being restrained by his government's responsiveness to British miasma and was avoiding any sole responsibility for blocking Israel's application. Sharett surmised that if France had been favourably disposed, then Canada would not have blocked the application; however, Canada would have borne part of the responsibility with France: "The matter hinged on France."[19] So a Franco-Canadian entente produced a compromise to defer the admission application for one month. Having failed to be adopted, the application was voted upon. Only Argentina, Columbia, the Ukraine, the United States, and the Soviet Union supported the recommendation; Syria opposed, and Belgium, Canada, China, France, and the United Kingdom abstained, and the membership application was rejected. Britain's quasi-negative influence held, but the anglophone-francophone entente's position could not be sustained lest British credibility be impaired. Britain in particular could not maintain its negative policy toward Israel.

With the adjournment of the United Nations session, it had now become quite clear that Canada itself could no longer procrastinate in its official stand on Israel's statehood. As Pearson was later to recall:

"In my speech to the First Committee of the Assembly on 22 November, I spoke in favour of limited recognition which was given in Ottawa on 24 December *with no demur from London.*"[20] Such was formally communicated by the Secretary of State for External Affairs to the Foreign Minister of the provisional Government of Israel. In fact the United Kingdom was to follow the Canadian recognition in a month's time.

At the start of 1949 the increased tension between Britain and Israel reached undisguised military confrontation. Canada's United Nations representative, General McNaughton, assumed the Security Council's presidency for the month of January. On 14 January Eban formally complained to McNaughton over British interpretations of the truce and of British troop movements which the Israeli representative regarded as a challenge to the Council. The "hysteria" in London was common knowledge, and McNaughton promised to check with Ottawa on the matter of British troop movements.[21]

Israel's United Nations representative Eban had remarked on McNaughton's cordiality which he ascribed to Canada's recent recognition. As previously noted, McNaughton had been regarded as one of Mackenzie King's trusted lieutenants, and the former prime minister had been more comfortable with him than with Pearson at the United Nations.[22] McNaughton's alternate, Ignatieff, unlike McNaughton, was less prone to British influence. According to Ignatieff, "St Laurent agreed with Pearson; McNaughton tended to side with the Arabs."[23]

Sharett had cited British truculence in cables to Commonwealth foreign ministers regarding Royal Air Force sorties over battle areas. "Such activities involving the Egyptian forces were leading to an undesirable and unwarranted crisis."[24] British Foreign Secretary Ernest Bevin's hostile attitude was having a deleterious effect on the domestic and international fronts. He was being subjected to severe criticism in the British parliament and press which pointed to the bankruptcy of his obdurate stand. The United Kingdom cabinet finally decided to temper the situation and grant *de facto* recognition on 18 January, a week prior to Israel's first general election. The official announcement was made on the 29th, four days after the election.

British *de facto* recognition was both related to recent events and part of a *quid pro quo* with the American administration. Since the British wanted to elevate its Transjordanian client's international standing, the United States agreed to recognition of the Hashemite Kingdom. In the interim, France maintained its own credibility and granted Israel *de facto* recognition on 24 January.

Israel continued to press Canada as well as other states – particularly Security Council members – on the admission issue. In February,

Elath visited Ottawa and was favourably impressed with his meetings with senior cabinet ministers, some officials, and some Liberal and CCF (Co-operative Commonwealth Federation Party) parliamentarians.[25] He remarked that Pearson was apologetic on Canada's vote at the Paris United Nations session in December, in which he had instructed R.G. "Gerry" Riddell not to vote for Israel's admission, indicating that the brakes had been put on the External Affairs minister. Elath found Defence Minister Brooke Claxton, Trade and Commerce Minister C.D. Howe agreeable, and United States Ambassador Lawrence Steinhardt helpful. That was also true of the two Jewish Liberal MPs (Members of Parliament), David Croll of Toronto (Spadina), and Maurice Hartt of Montreal (Cartier). He did, however, specifically mention CCF leader M.J. Coldwell and CCF foreign affairs spokesperson Alistair Stewart – the latter representing the sizeable Jewish populated constituency of Winnipeg North – as "very friendly."[26]

The Canadian bureaucracy responded coldly to Elath. According to Elath External Affairs Under-Secretary Escott Reid was unfriendly, his views probably having been influenced by the pro-Arab Elizabeth Mac-Callum.[27] Still, policy was the minister's decision, and he and Eban felt assured that Canada's vote for admission to the United Nations would be positive barring any "new attack by us."[28] Moreover Eban felt confident that success in the February armistice talks (between Egypt and Israel) would probably remove any hesitation on Ottawa's part.[29]

Canada's intention to push for a vote on 4 March again fell subject to British pressure designed to delay Israel's membership.[30] Israel's tack was to urge the Canadians to protect British prestige, since the latter intended to abstain. What had appeared to be an unshakeable Canadian support become somewhat muted.[31] Yet knowledge that British forces were still moving about the region and causing considerable embarrassment incensed the Americans and now especially the Canadians.[32] No one wanted a repeat of the 7 January incident when Israeli fighter aircraft downed five British military planes which had crossed over into Israeli-held territory originally assigned to the proposed Jewish state. Ignatieff strove to convince the British to be more receptive and fall into line.[33]

On another matter, Israel was disappointed and somewhat miffed at Canada's abstention on the vote for Israel's participation in the International Wheat Conference as well as its negative vote on Israel's participation in the Food and Agriculture Organization's (FAO) conference.[34] Canada's votes were particularly important in view of its position as one of the world's major grain and food producers.

The seriousness of Israel's application was given greater attention during April, when the Security Council finally recommended Israel's admission to membership. Pearson specifically instructed the Canadian delegation not to oppose Israel's application in the UN General Committee. The External Affairs minister was concerned about (1) Israel and Jerusalem and the Holy Places; (2) finding the late United Nations mediator Count Bernadotte's assassins;[35] and (3) Israel's responsibility regarding the Palestinian refugees.[36] On 27 April Pearson cabled Arnold D.P. Heeney, the new High Commissioner in London, that support should be given to the United Nations General Committee's reference to Israel's application to the Ad Hoc Committee. He also noted that he had no objection to sponsoring a resolution to admit Israel providing that sponsorship included respectable states like Australia and the United States.[37]

Canada on 6 May joined Australia, Guatemala, Haiti, Panama, Uruguay, and the United States in sponsoring an admission resolution in the Ad Hoc Committee. At that time, there were many telegrams drawing attention to the Argentinian and Greek-Saudi proposals about the Holy See's concerns which sought to delay Israel's admission. The St Laurent government demurred and abstained from the Argentine sponsored proposals, but the Canadian co-sponsored resolution on Israel's admission was carried in the General Assembly's plenary session on 11 May.

With the passage of the resolution and Israel's admission to United Nations membership, Canada had granted implied *de jure* recognition. In a letter Pearson notified fellow Liberal MP Maurice Hartt that full recognition then existed.[38] That was subsequently confirmed by Pearson in a 19 August 1949 communication on the subject to Sharett, who acknowledged it on 11 October.[39]

With full recognition of Israel, the word Palestine did not entirely fade. Canada never recognized Transjordan's annexation of eastern Palestine, also called the West Bank or Judaea and Samaria, hereafter the territories: the United Kingdom and Pakistan were the only states to do so. Use of the term Palestine was to be explained by Jean Lesage, then parliamentary assistant to the External Affairs minister, when responding to fellow Liberal MP Leon Crestohl's question about the term. Lesage stated on 25 March 1952 that "the word Palestine referred to the country on both sides of the Jordan":[40] (in its historical and quasi-legal connotation that remains valid). Moreover, the Gaza strip controlled by Egypt was never recognized as part of Egyptian territory.

Israel now began to move to increase and consolidate its diplomatic relations. Comay requested that Elath inform the Canadian government during his February 1949 visit to Ottawa of Israel's desire to establish a consulate.[41] One of the Jewish-Canadian community's leaders, D. Lou Harris, informed Arthur Lourie of Israel's Foreign

Ministry that the consul should speak "the language as well as the natives, and understand the behaviour and manners just as well as the natives do themselves."[42] The request might have been the desire for a cloned Canadian, but the intent was at least for a native anglophone. The appointee was English-born Avraham Harman, then with the Press and Information division of Israel's Foreign Ministry.[43] Elath was requested to obtain Canadian approval of Harman's appointment as Israel's first consul general in Canada.[44]

At the beginning of March, Pearson had indicated, "I think they [Israelis] should be permitted to go ahead with their consular appointment as soon as they are admitted to the United Nations. Until that time they could send us a consular agent if they so desire – there is a precedent for this in their representation in Washington prior to *de jure* recognition."[45] Actual notification was designed to coincide with Israel's admittance to the United Nations. As consul general to Canada, Harman was to be stationed in Montreal due to its proximity to the nation's capital and because it housed the country's largest Jewish community and was headquarters for the major Jewish organizations. In July Harman arrived to assume his duties accompanied by Arie Ben-Tovim as consul. The official appointment had been preceded by United Zionist Council of Canada chairman S.J. "Sam" Zacks, meeting with Pearson and Under-Secretary Arnold Heeney in late March. On 1 April Hume Wrong, Canada's ambassador in Washington, communicated with Elath, and Harman's appointment was formalized on 25 May.

With Israeli's diplomatic status formally inaugurated, the Canadian government felt impelled to maintain an equilibrium with the Arab states. The Lebanese consulate in Ottawa was raised to consulate general, and in mid-December the government agreed to the opening of an Egyptian consulate general in Ottawa as well. As to the reception of the Israeli diplomats, Harman noted that the External Affairs people did not accord the consul general "the same informal diplomatic status which is the practice with us."[46] That apparently applied to the other non-Israelis, so Harman cautioned that Israel should move slowly.

Israel's next move to advance its status was to seek the level of legation. In his 24 February report Elath had stressed the need to develop friendly relations with Canada because of its growing importance in international affairs, and called for the opening of an embassy after the receipt of *de jure* recognition. In subsequent discussions the Israeli Foreign Ministry's Director General, Walter Eytan, communicated with Heeney that Israel desired to establish a legation in Ottawa headed by an envoy extraordinaire and minister plenipotentiary.[47]

The Canadians were in no great hurry to raise Israel's diplomatic level. Comay felt that if the legation proposal were accepted, then Israel might press for a reciprocal act by Canada. Indeed St Laurent, under pressure from the Catholic Church – especially over the issue of the internationalization of Jerusalem – was also opposed to any reciprocity at that time. In July he had expressed that there would certainly be objections to having representation in Israel and not in the Vatican. The lack of direct Canadian diplomatic relations with the Holy See had been a cause for chagrin among Catholics.[48] That in turn could lead to pressure by the Egyptians and Lebanese for such similar action. Hence the cautious Canadians had to be assured that the Israelis would not pursue reciprocity.[49] Comay wanted higher diplomatic relations with all the "older Dominions," and urged Eban to discuss the matter with Canadians in Washington because Pearson was apparently too busy. Eban promised to take up the matter with Pearson at United Nations Lake Success (New York) headquarters. This was followed by subsequent communications with the Washington embassy's first secretary, M. Yuval, who stated that he would go to Ottawa to "emphasize again that no request of reciprocity is involved in the opening of a Legation in Ottawa."[50] Yet Comay was still apprehensive that a legation "will involve them in obligations towards the Arabs."[51] Nevertheless by the following February Pearson informed Eban that he would now welcome an Israeli minister in Ottawa. The Canadian cabinet approved the notion with the proviso that Canada would not be able to reciprocate for some time.[52]

Comay then informed Yuval that the candidate would have to be (a) of high calibre to match those from other foreign missions in Ottawa; (b) conscious of Canadian-United States ties; (c) aware of Canadian-United Kingdom and Commonwealth ties; (d) interested in the United Nations; (e) able to participate in the Jewish community in Ottawa and to help the national Canadian Jewish Congress and the Zionist Organization of Canada. Within budgetary and personnel limitation, there would be a commercial counsellor or attache and a secretary for press and non-Jewish groups. Contacts with the Jewish communities would be carried out by the Montreal consul general. The military attaché in Washington could be accredited to Ottawa if approved.[53]

A minor oversight occurred during this period, which was diplomatically innocuous but is noteworthy in a humorous historical perspective. Y. Meroz of the Israeli foreign ministry remarked to Yuval that he wanted to apologize for forgetting Good Friday in Ottawa and hoped that External Affairs didn't mind: "After all to use [a] permanent excuse – this is the first legation in Canada in two thousand years."[54]

Only in 1953 was action finally taken. Comay was nominated to head the Ottawa mission. Hume Wrong informed Eban that the Canadian government agreed to Comay's appointment as envoy extraordinaire and minister plenipotentiary. President Yitzchak Ben Zvi's letter of credence was signed on 12 June. Comay arrived on 1 September and presented his credentials to the acting Governor-General, Supreme Court Justice Locke.[55]

The question of a prospective Jewish-Canadian diplomat accredited to Israel now arose. MP David Croll, former Ontario Minister of Labour and a retired lieutenant colonel, had been mooted as a possible candidate. Croll had felt chagrined at not having received a cabinet portfolio due, many felt, to St Laurent's inability to appoint a Jew in spite of Croll's unquestionable political and geographic credentials. His name had also come up for the Israeli posting, perhaps because of his affiliation with the Labour Zionist movement. Israel's Foreign Ministry felt such an appointment at the ambassadorial level would best be filled by a non-Jew. The designated appointee would not be placed in the position of being a "super-patriot" and hyper-critical of Israel to prove he was "unswervingly loyal."[56] Director-General Eytan, however, noted the necessity not to discriminate against a Jew and hence have to keep "mum."[57]

The Israeli director-general also raised with Comay the matter of the unwelcome prospect of diplomatic representation by a non-resident ambassador. Since Canadian representation was probably going to be linked to the Ankara or Athens embassy, Eytan preferred Athens because all other nations had linked Israel to their Ankara embassies, which risked Israel's coming to be regarded as an appendage to Turkey. Moreover, an appointment from Athens could help to increase Israeli links with Greece. As for the embassy in Israel; if the Canadians wanted it in Tel Aviv as opposed to the Jerusalem capital where the Israelis desired it, then so be it. It was better than nothing at all. In that regard Eytan cited an old Yiddish adage: "Besser a Yid ohn a bord, eyder a bord ohn a Yid" (Better a Jew without a beard than a beard without a Jew)."[58] The unbearded Tel Aviv embassy became the reality.

Another possible complication concerned the prospect of a non-resident Ambassador acquiring seniority within the diplomatic corps; hence making it conceivable that the non-resident would become doyen of the diplomatic corps. Such a possibility, while unlikely, could create some discomfort were it to occur. As for the actual incumbent, Israeli officialdom still preferred a non-Jewish career diplomat.[59]

Other than at Ankara, there had been no Canadian diplomatic representation in the Middle East before 1954. The time was also ripe for ambassadorial exchanges with Israel. During the summer of 1954 that was formalized. The Canadian Ambassador in Athens, T.W.L. (Terry) MacDermott, was appointed non-resident ambassador with George Kidd as chargé d'affaires in Tel Aviv.[60] Prudentially maintaining the balance with the Arab states, there was a simultaneous announcement of Canadian missions to Beirut and Cairo.[61] The Egyptians also opened an embassy in Ottawa, and the Lebanese added a consulate which was also to take charge of Iraqi interests in Canada. Comay's rank was raised to ambassador and the legation's to embassy.

In June of 1956, Comay wrote to Eytan and Arthur Lourie that it was time to remind the Canadian government that it had no resident ambassador. Cautiously, Eytan advised Comay to be patient and wait if not asked.[62] Some eleven months later, Canadian Jewish Congress president Samuel Bronfman and United Zionist Council chairman Michael Garber submitted a brief to Pearson which called for the upgrading of relations to an ambassador in residence.[63] The June 1957 election swept the longtime Liberal government from power and brought in a minority Progressive Conservative government headed by John Diefenbaker. The outspoken pro-Israel new prime minister won a landslide majority in the following 31 March 1958 election. In September 1958 he appointed career diplomat Margaret Meagher Canada's first resident ambassador.

The cautious decade concluded with the residential appointment in Tel Aviv. In spite of Diefenbaker's pro-Israel credentials, the embassy and offices stayed close to the Mediterranean shoreline, still a distance from the capital in the Judaean hills. Diefenbaker never moved the embassy to Jerusalem, but persisted in calling for such action when he returned to the opposition benches in the 1960s. To this day, Tel Aviv remains the site of the embassy's offices, while the move to Jerusalem is in abeyance.

2 The Non-internationalization of Jerusalem

Jerusalem, hallowed by the world's three major monotheistic religions, again survived an alien conqueror when the British withdrew on 14 May 1948. In accordance with the United Nations partition resolution, the city and its environs was to be administered as a demilitarized and neutral zone under UN auspices. An international political entity was envisaged within the partition plan's economic union for the separate Arab and Jewish states. The designated administrator was to be a United Nations governor operating under a special statute drafted by and responsible to the Trusteeship Council. The council's April 1948 draft statute for Jerusalem turned out to be ineffective in the light of the military struggle then in progress between Arab and Jewish forces.

Addressing the General Assembly's Third Committee on 22 November 1948, Pearson called for a reaffirmation of "the recommendation it had previously made that there should be international control of Jerusalem, and should call upon both parties to cooperate in implementing this recommendation."[1] On 11 December the General Assembly adopted Resolution A-194 whereby the Palestine Conciliation Commission was established to deal with Jerusalem and its environs as well as the Holy Places, including Nazareth. France, Turkey, and the United States composed the commission.

The Palestine Conciliation Commission was unsuccessful in its attempts to gain Israeli and Jordanian agreement for an internationalization plan encompassing the Jerusalem area. Reality had dictated a sense of modification over internationalization because any approach to the problem had to take into account the Arab and Jewish populated zones. Canada took the position that the General Assembly should avoid debating questions with which the Palestine Conciliation Commission was dealing. On 12 September 1949 the commission's plan was finally published which recognized that the Arab and Jewish zones would provide for their own municipal administrations coupled with a mixed body dealing with transport and communications. A United Nations commissioner would oversee protection of the Holy Places, demilitarization, and freedom of access, and there was to be a tribunal as well as a mixed court for the settlement of disputes.

United Nations circles did not find the plan palatable, and Canada was less than enthusiastic. In a cable to Moshe Sharett, Abba Eban gave a brief report on his two talks with Pearson. He noted that Pearson "admits to heavy Catholic pressure [in] Canada but states that leaves him cold, as only concern[ed] religious groups should be for safeguarding the Holies. Future government [of] Jerusalem is a political matter, and not their business. If safeguarding Holies can be done with consent [of] those involved, Canada [is] not prepared [to] sacrifice this consent for [an] ambitious policy to be imposed. Secondly, he said: (1) Jerusalem shouldn't be discussed at all [in the] Security Council; (2) General Assembly should take such steps as necessary for protection [of] Holies."[2] Pragmatism was the guideline for Canada inasmuch as full internationalization was regarded as beyond possibility (notwithstanding concerted Vatican pressure through the Catholic hierarchy – especially in Quebec – which sought as full a degree of internationalization of Jerusalem and its environs as possible).

Those who demurred from total internationalization felt that Israel and Jordan – the latter then not a member of the United Nations – should exercise their respective full jurisdictional powers and reach agreement with the United Nations on safeguards to protect the Holy Places. Canada found itself in the "middle" school, which was not prepared to grant full powers to the occupiers but preferred what came to be known as functional internationalization, that is, granting Israel and Jordan secular control while a modified form of internationalization protected the outside world's religious interests.

Australia – itself under considerable Catholic pressure with an election in the offing – proposed a resolution as amended by El Salvador, the Soviet Union, and Lebanon for a *corpus separatum*. It was adopted by the General Assembly on 9 December by a vote of 38 to 14, with 7 abstentions. Canada cast one of the negative votes along with the United States and United Kingdom because it preferred the Dutch-Swedish proposal for functional internationalization, which would have left secular interests to Israel and Jordan while limiting international control strictly for the Holy Places. Its opposition to the Australian-sponsored resolution was predicated on the belief that effective United Nations control of the Holy Places should avoid unnecessary roles. As General McNaughton noted in his statement to the General Assembly prior to the vote, "Such unnecessary responsibilities, if beyond the powers of the United Nations, would be inadequately discharged. Such a situation would place the Holy Places and the interests of religious persons throughout the world in jeopardy."[3]

Thus the Canadian delegation cast its negative vote notwithstanding the Holy See's pressure on a government headed by a Catholic and an adamant francophone press supporting full internationalization. In the run-up to the General Assembly vote, the major Canadian francophone newspapers called for support of the Catholic viewpoint based upon the Pontiff's position. That was expressed in the influential *Le Soleil* (Quebec City) of 9 November and *Le Devoir* (Montreal) on 10 November, and by L.P. Roy of *L'Action catholique* (Quebec City) on 23 November, calling for strong support for the Australian draft resolution. Among the editorialists in the anglophone press, the government's position found greater support. That was the case with the Liberal-leaning *The Citizen* (Ottawa), and I. Norman Smith of the Progressive Conservative-leaning *The Ottawa Journal.*[4] *The Globe and Mail* (Toronto) of 28 November did not want the United Nations to become just a bystander, the position it deduced from Sharett's position.

Assessments by external affairs personnel indicate their pragmatic approach. Under-Secretary Arnold Heeney indicated in a memorandum of 5 December for the minister that appointment of Israel and Jordan as administering authorities with a resident United Nations commissioner for advisory work "is probably wise for an organization which does not possess executive power and is committed to reforms without interference in the internal affairs of member states."[5] That same day McNaughton informed the minister that he proposed to vote for a milder Dutch-Swedish proposal but would probably abstain in the sub-committee.[6]

In the Commons Pearson stated that Canada had abstained "on the ground that it was not satisfied the plan could be carried out effectively."[7] Also on the 5th, Eban wrote Pearson seeking his support for a negative vote on the Australian proposal.[8] In the Ad Hoc's sub-committee, the Australian draft was opposed by the United Kingdom, the United States, and the then non-member Jordan. India as well as Canada abstained, and as Pearson later claimed, "It was not opposed to the principle enunciated but thought the proposal unrealistic." Adopted measures, he said, had to "be practicable and enforceable." Pearson also noted that had the partition plan been realized as originally passed on 29 November 1947, it would have been easier for the

Jewish authorities to accept internationalization. As it happened, the Australian-proposed resolution was based on the 1947 partition plan.[9]

Concern over reaction to this vote was expected in a country whose population was 40 percent Roman Catholic. Realizing that it would be expedient to have a measured public response, the prime minister's office prepared a form letter to explain its negative vote. The letter noted with regret that the majority of United Nations delegates were not for the reasonable Dutch-Swedish proposal but instead opted for a resolution which could prove detrimental to the Holy Places simply because Israel and Jordan were opposed to it.[10] The External Affairs minister requested that the United Nations delegation try to avoid involvement over the Jerusalem issue if it came up at the Security Council where Canada was completing its two-year term.[11]

Although the francophone press was clearly upset by the government's vote, it still urged carrying out the Australian-sponsored resolution and accepting the majority decision.[12] The anglophone press reaction was in sharp contrast to its French-Canadian counterparts. *The Citizen* of 12 December thought the internationalization of Jerusalem was unnecessary; on the 14th the *Winnipeg Free Press*, another independent liberal paper, agreed but chided the government for having been "timorous and equivocal." Pat Conroy, secretary-treasurer of the Canadian Congress of Labour, who had just returned from a trip to Israel, wrote Heeney that the internationalization proposal was not practical. He believed that a treaty between Israel and Jordan should be concluded with the United Nations supervising the Holy Places.[13]

In an attempt to placate the disgruntled Canadian Catholic hierarchy, Leon Mayrand of External Affairs, who had been Justice Ivan Rand's alternate on the United Nations Special Committee on Palestine (UNSCOP), called on Monsignor Alexandre Vachon, Archbishop of Ottawa. He also spoke with C. L'Herioux of *Le Droit* (Ottawa), which was owned by the Oblate Fathers, and with Father Barthelemy of the Commission for the Holy Land in Ottawa. Nevertheless, the Church's officials were not assuaged and remained upset that Canada's vote was contrary to the Holy Father's wishes.[14]

As requested by the Australian resolution, the Trusteeship Council began the task of updating the Statute of Jerusalem, which had been neglected since May 1948. Although Canada had abstained in committee on the matter of an $8 million appropriation for the international regime of Jerusalem, it now voted in favour of that provision.

As a result of the General Assembly decision, Israel moved ahead to assert its claim to western Jerusalem. On 13 December, Israel's unicameral parliament, the Knesset, voted to transfer the seat of government from Tel Aviv to Jerusalem. Calling for a revocation of the

Israeli act, the Trusteeship Council communicated its demand on 20 December. Eban's response to Roger Garreau, the Trusteeship Council president and French representative, was to state that the call for revocation was "extra-Charter" as far as responsibilities were concerned. He chided the council that it was diverting "from its high mission for the advancement of backward territories and peoples towards self-government and independence, towards a needless attempt to cancel the liberty already achieved by the population of Jerusalem."[15] An External Affairs memorandum of 4 January 1950 duly noted the Israeli action and expressed the hope that the first consideration should be for the Holy Places.[16]

The Canadian government's scepticism over effective internationalization of Jerusalem remained undiminished. An external affairs *aide-mémoire* cautioned that if the Trusteeship Council found its task impossible, then the Canadian observer at Geneva "should express no opinion." Instructions were for him to observe "and not for the purpose of engaging in discussions of policy."[17] Such prudence seemed wise to avoid further chagrined feelings. Nevertheless, a further note two days later suggested that at the forthcoming press conference on the question of the Knesset's move to Jerusalem, an answer be given that it did not appear possible for the United Nations to work out a plan; however, anything which was possible should be given sympathetic consideration.[18]

On 4 April the Trusteeship Council approved its statute for Jerusalem. That it essentially embodied a United Nations-controlled separate political entity doomed it to failure. Neither Israel nor Jordan would accept it, and by mid-June the council decided to report back to the General Assembly. In the interim, the Israeli government on 26 May submitted a proposal to Garreau in which the practical approach resembled the Canadian government's attitude. As *The Montreal Star* remarked in its editorial of 31 May referring to McNaughton's statement of 9 December, "The Israeli proposal is virtually on all fours with the proposal made by Canada to the General Assembly." *The Citizen* had similar praise two days later. Yet the *Winnipeg Free Press* of 29 April was more critical of the Canadian government's policy: "Canada has played a barren role in this controversy until now. It should take a more active part in the next Assembly in September in arranging a practical and workable settlement." It did, however, remark that in view of Jordan's annexation of the old city and Arab-held Palestine, the plan for Jerusalem's internationalization should be abandoned followed by negotiations between Israel and Jordan for protection of and accessibility to the Holy Places.

In a meeting of minds, Eban wrote to Gerry Riddell about Canada's "constructive and realistic attitude" taken during the General Assembly's Fourth Session (1949). He requested a consultation on the plan for a United Nations authority for the Holy Places.[19] Eban believed that "a final solution to the Jerusalem problem could be found if a group of like minded delegations would join in 'sponsorship.'"[20]

Noting the shift in attitudes, and conscious of the opinions of the Catholic Church, External Affairs wanted its reactions to developments. On 28 June, External Affairs' C.S.A. Ritchie informed the Canadian ambassador in Rome of the attitudinal shifts regarding the Trusteeship Council's plan; yet the Vatican seemed adamant. Ritchie further noted that Leon Mayrand had spoken with Archbishop Alexandre Vachon and L'Herioux of Le Droit regarding the Vatican's disposition. Elizabeth MacCallum had prepared a memorandum for External Affairs' European divisional heads pointing out that there now appeared a strong undercurrent in the Vatican to modify its position on the internationalization issue. While there was to be a consideration for suggestions, it appeared premature at that stage to have discussed sponsorship of resolutions.[21] A further memorandum recommended that the government keep free of commitments.[22]

Even the notion of a Vatican-type state for Jerusalem was not regarded as feasible. In a conversation with Eugene Cardinal Tisserant, External Affairs' Jules Léger reported that it appeared that part of the Curia was opposed to Vatican policy and opposition to any workable plan was then less pronounced.[23]

With the General Assembly going into session, the evolving Canadian foreign policy tradition of reconciling divergent views was again an option. There was a feeling that perhaps a United Nations authority for the Holy Places was probably the best prospect to garner support. The concept of a diarchic regime still retained some appeal and had Canadian support at the last General Assembly session. Moreover, the minister felt that Israel and Jordan might acquiesce in such arrangements.[24]

By November hesitancy had re-emerged. Enquiries were made of the Vatican's disposition from the ambassador to France. Caution again came to the fore and Canada objected to sponsoring resolutions as evidence surfaced that Israel and Jordan were not amenable. Furthermore, the Vatican was still obstinate on its full internationalization stand; the Latin Americans would not accept anything with which the Holy See was not in accord, and prospects were not bright after the meetings Mayrand had held with the Dutch, French, Swedish, United Kingdom, and United States representatives at the United Nations.[25]

By mid-December, an impasse in the adoption of a General Assembly resolution appeared unavoidable. A Swedish proposal for a modified form of international control through a United Nations commission for the Holy Places did not move. On 15 December a Belgian draft to name four persons to study United Nations supervision of the Holy Places and spiritual and religious interests failed to achieve a two-thirds majority. Canada abstained because it had come to doubt the utility of additional enquiries after Israel and Jordan had made their positions clear: they, however, voluntarily pledged to allow freedom of access and the maintenance of the rights of religious denominations. Mayrand's note to Elizabeth MacCallum succinctly summarized the Canadian position, as Pearson "told me to keep one eye on Jerusalem and the other on Quebec." Hence the silence and the abstention.[26]

Canada's quandary and its sensitivity to the Catholic Church's feelings over the matter was apparently sufficient to deter a suggested visit some four months later by the Israeli prime minister to Canada. Pearson had informed Canadian Jewish Congress president Samuel Bronfman and MP Leon Crestohl that a visit by Prime Minister David Ben Gurion to the United States would not be extended to Canada because of the duress Prime Minister St Laurent was experiencing. The Canadian prime minister did not want any more attention drawn to either the Jerusalem issue or Canada's lack of an official envoy to the Vatican. It was deemed that a visit by Ben Gurion would not only draw attention but would put unwanted pressure on the Canadian government.[27]

Attempts to resolve the internationalization issue were beginning to recede. Israel considered the General Assembly's recommendations on the subject dated and impossible. Reality was gaining centre stage, and less complex resolutions designed to sustain the Conciliation Commission's work were coming forth. In an effort to gain Arab and Israeli consent, Canada proposed eliminating references to the implementation of past General Assembly resolutions and merely recalling them in the preambles. An amended resolution was subsequently adopted on 26 January 1952 which called upon the parties to accept responsibility for reaching a settlement and for the Conciliation Commission to continue to be available to assist in the settlement of outstanding issues.[28]

At the United Nations General Assembly's seventh session, which convened in October 1952, the Conciliation Commission's review was presented to the Ad Hoc Political Committee. This time, however, the Conciliation Commission did not present a resolution. The issue was concerned with direct negotiations, which was Israel's preference but which the Arabs still spurned. A resolution to that effect received a two-thirds majority in the committee but failed to be adopted by the plenum. Similarly, a Philippine amendment more akin to the Arab stance, presented on 18 December, also failed to be adopted. It had called for the internationalization of Jerusalem but avoided the notion of direct negotiations. Canada opposed the avoidance of direct negotiations and abstained on the internationalization issue, holding to its position that the Trusteeship Council's statute was inoperable. In that respect, Canada and Israel had a meeting of minds on direct negotiations for the pacific settlement of disputes.[29]

By the autumn of 1953 External Affairs' MacCallum noted that the Vatican might now support a temporary arrangement for functional internationalization. Ottawa was careful to check with London and Washington before moving on any ideas. One such notion concerned the possibility of appointing the Knights of St John (Malta), to supervise the Holy Places.[30]

Ambassadorial-level exchanges complicated Canada's position. External Affairs was concerned not to compromise its stand on non-recognition of Jerusalem as Israel's capital, specifically the presentation of diplomatic credentials.[31] The protocol division was informed that ambassador-designate Terry MacDermott was to present his credentials at the Israeli president's residence in Jerusalem. It was also to be the case with the chargé d'affaires, George Kidd. External affairs did not want to attract any attention and avoided giving press attention.[32] Moreover, the traditional proffering of messages on the presentation of credentials would have to be accorded to the presidents of Egypt and Lebanon. Hence there was caution to be bland, since special messages "attract attention."[33] In fact no messages was the preference.

Anticipating Arab protests, the minister asked the embassies in Ankara, Athens, London, Tel Aviv, and Washington and the representative at the United Nations to explain that credentials are always presented where the chief of state resides.[34] On 24 November 1954 MacDermott presented his credentials to President Yitzchak Ben Zvi without any adverse results. The government's apprehension was allayed as R.A.D. Ford of External Affairs noted that the presentation in Jerusalem has "passed unnoticed in Arab circles."[35] External affairs relief from such over caution was best expressed through its publication of a picture of MacDermott presenting his credentials to Ben Zvi and in the same publication a picture of MacCallum, the new chargé d'affaires at the Beirut legation, presenting her credentials to Lebanese foreign minister Alfred Naccache.[36]

Further guidelines were prescribed by Under-Secretary Léger for the chargé d'affaires in Tel Aviv. He stated that occasional visits at the chancery level to the Foreign Ministry in Jerusalem were in order but no attendance at formal social functions. Private visits and the president's reception on Independence Day were permissible. Above all discretion had to be used.[37]

Israel's desire to enhance Jerusalem's diplomatic status and to draw more diplomats to the capital resulted in reduction of its Tel Aviv liaison office functions. The King David Hotel in Jerusalem became an acceptable venue for luncheon meetings of a diplomatic nature.[38] External affairs legal advisor, Max Wershoff, advised the European division – which covered Israel – that any enquiry by a Canadian citizen in Jerusalem should be referred to the United Kingdom Consul General there and to the Canadian Embassy in Tel Aviv.[39]

In another directive to Kidd, Léger advised: "I believe you should continue to resist as tactfully as possible efforts by the Israeli authorities to persuade you to abandon the idea of occasional visits by them to Tel Aviv," noting that perhaps Canada's influence in Israel was greater than that of other middle or small powers due to its role in the establishment of Israel, ties between Israel and the Jewish community in Canada, and Canada's fulfilment of some of Israel's military requests. He added: "If you see an opportunity to do so, explain to the Israeli authorities that the Canadian position on Jerusalem is in no sense doctrinaire and is related to firmly held beliefs in Canada."[40] The prudent non-committal stance was being maintained.

Following the Israeli elections on 26 July 1955, Ben Gurion resumed the premiership, replacing his earlier successor, Moshe Sharett. With the indefatigable Ben Gurion back, external affairs wanted it understood that there was to be no confusion over Canada's stand on Jerusalem.[41] Even babies born to Canadian parents in Jerusalem were to be registered as being born in Jerusalem and not Jerusalem, Israel.[42] While arrangements to meet the foreign minister in Jerusalem could be made, there had to be reciprocal visits in Tel Aviv. In any respect, the Tel Aviv embassy was advised to co-ordinate its actions with the American and British embassies.[43]

Well beyond the end of the decade, Canada's position on Jerusalem was not altered. It was based on quasi-reality with cautious regard for Israeli and Jordanian claims to sovereignty which would not be countenanced outside United Nations endorsement. As was noted in the previous chapter, matters did not change with the accession to power of the Progressive Conservatives under John Diefenbaker in June 1957 (reconfirmed in his government's landslide victory of March 1958). Neither Diefenbaker nor his successors took any steps to alter Canada's position on the Jerusalem embassy or its *de jure* recognition as Israel's capital even following Israel's taking of the eastern part of the city and its environs in the June 1967 Six Day War.

Matters seemed to change with the federal election of June 1979. Progressive Conservative leader Joe Clark tried to keep his pledge to move the embassy to Jerusalem if the party won the election, but the prospect of his fulfilling his pledge created a major controversy among various pressure groups especially in the business community. The prime minister backtracked under the guise of a special one-man enquiry headed by his predecessor as party leader, Robert Stanfield. The enquiry resulted in a negative recommendation concerning the move.[44]

The first decade, like the following ones, concluded with Israel's sovereignty over Jerusalem unrecognized and with the embassy still a stone's throw from the Mediterranean and tens of kilometres away from Israel's capital.

3 Aiding the Palestinian Refugee

Israel's war of independence also resulted in the displacement of Arabs and Jews from sovereign and non-sovereign Arab lands extending from the Maghreb of North Africa in the west to the Persian Gulf in the east. A resolution has yet to be found for the claims of Jews from Arab countries and the Arab-Palestinians for compensation, and in the latter case for resettlement. While Israel absorbed the bulk of the Jewish refugees from Arab countries, the Arab-Palestinians posed an ongoing and seemingly intractable problem. Whatever the political vicissitudes, Canada and other United Nations members only concerned themselves with the Palestinians. Many believed that the United Nations and its refugee relief agency should be the major administrator in dealing with the refugees' circumstances. From the outset the Canadian government decided that material support was the most practical means of ameliorating the Palestinians' plight and would be a principal actor in supporting United Nations endeavours. Indeed, Canada became the fourth largest contributor.

Although the Palestinian refugee issue did not adversely affect Canadian policy toward Israel during the first decade, it remained one aspect in the bilateral relationship insofar as Canada wanted a greater response by Israel in addressing the issue. The Palestinian issue remained an ongoing Canadian concern particularly in the aftermath of the prime ministerships of Diefenbaker and Pearson in the post-1968 era, when Canadian governments became more critical of Israeli activities in Gaza and the territories, where most of the Palestinian refugees lived.

The Canadian government's first reaction to the issue was in the prime minister's response to British Foreign Secretary Ernest Bevin's request to support the refugees. St Laurent felt that it was impossible to do anything for them unless it was part of a United Nations scheme.[1] A month later, the General Assembly's resolution of 11 December called for the return of the refugees to their homes and compensation for those not wishing to return.[2]

Canada's initial contributions were made through the Canadian Red Cross, by arrangement with the United Nations International Children's Emergency Fund (UNICEF), and through United Nations relief for Palestinian refugees. Canada subsequently voted for the establishment of the Relief and Works Agency (UNWRA) in the General Assembly resolution of 8 December 1949 whose first director was General Howard Kennedy of Canada. The Canadian contribution amounted to $750,000, and Canada was also appointed a member of the negotiating committee to secure commitments from the member states for the agency.

The government's attitude in the matter was to confine the issue to states *per se* and it objected to the inclusion of the Arab Higher Committee and the Arab League. Moreover, External Affairs wanted the General Assembly to recognize that resettlement in Arab lands as well as repatriation to Israel would be the basis for liquidating the refugee problem.[3]

John Blanchford of the United States, who succeeded Kennedy, presented a $250 million assistance program for a three-year period beginning 1 July 1951. The Canadian government supported the program but reserved the right to decide its contributions. If, however, there were no progress on conciliatory matters, External Affairs officials felt, ironically, given subsequent events, "We would probably be prepared to support proposals based on the more realistic premise that a settlement of the refugee problem must precede a peace settlement."[4]

The St Laurent government still held to the position that broader financial responses were needed from members who voted for resolutions but had made no financial contributions.[5] In the first week of July 1952, Parliament approved a $600 thousand contribution, still wanting to see other contributions come forward in comparative terms. Although that did not occur, Canada maintained its level in subsequent years, between half and three quarters of a million dollars.

Although Canada's contributions could be regarded as admirable, the issue remained insoluble. It was clear that any non-treaty settlement remained impossible. In Parliament there were rare references as to whether Canada was doing all it could to admit refugees of Arab origin.[6] In his appearance before the Commons Standing Committee on External Affairs, Pearson expressed his concern over the non-rehabilitation of Palestinian refugees. Noting that there could hardly be peace in the absence of Israel's neighbours' recognizing its existence, he nevertheless called upon the Jewish state to assist in removing fears of its "aggressive" stance "by making a constructive contribution to the refugee problem."[7] When questioned by Stanley Knowles of the CCF of his use of the term "aggressive," the minister repented, admitting that it had a bad connotation and he should have said "progressive."[8]

Pearson believed that the Arab states were doing little for those refugees and also called for an Israeli contribution, even a token one, for its great psychological value. On 7 June 1955 Ambassador Comay reported that Pearson had asked him that Israel show some token repatriation, "even if we found it more convenient to call it family reunion or something else."[9]

In subsequent Commons debates, Alistair Stewart of the CCF noted the desperate poverty of those refugees and criticized the Arab nations for using them as pawns and indoctrinating them with hatred. Regarding Israel's spurned offer to take back a hundred thousand, Stewart could not see Israel taking back a massive number who might try to destroy the state. That would be "asking more than any modern state would be prepared to accede to."[10] In his statement to the Commons on 24 January 1956, the External Affairs minister noted that Canada had contributed its fair share and stated: "As I see it, some compensation should be paid these refugees by Israel for loss of land and home. But it is clear that so large a number cannot return to their former land ... A limited amount of repatriation might be possible such as that which would be involved, for example, in the reuniting of families. For the rest, resettlement as an international operation, to which Israel among others would make a contribution, seems to be the only answer."[11]

During the same debate, Social Credit member A.B. Patterson called for the money for the Arab refugees to be used for their rehabilitation. Noting that some had been accepted and rehabilitated into the Israeli economy, he said, "I do not think it is too much to suggest that those who remain should now become the responsibility of the Arab countries."[12]

As for domestic policy, the Canadian government had tentatively decided to admit a limited number of Palestinian refugees as immigrants. The refugees were to be chosen among English and French speakers in Jordan and Lebanon who had specified skills and trades who could "also meet certain health and other requirements."[13] It was intended to be a modest gesture.

The events in the wake of the Sinai-Suez conflict in the autumn of 1956 indicated a unique Canadian approach to one aspect of the Arab refugee problem. As a preliminary approach, External Affairs' John Holmes on 20 February 1957 addressed the General Assembly's Special Committee. He praised the United Nations Relief and Works Agency and the need to support it. The problem, he stated, would be, "if not solved, at least greatly alleviated."[14] In a balanced manner he expressed his disappointment that Israel had not offered some repatriation and compensation to the neighbouring countries for not having seen fit to support rehabilitation and resettlement schemes. Noting that Canada was the fourth largest contributor to relief efforts (having contributed nearly $5.5 million), he further regretted "the problem posed by the attitude on some matters of some host governments."[15] He stressed the agonizing plight of the refugees of the Gaza strip.

In his 26 February address to the General Assembly, Pearson proposed a quasi-United Nations administration for the Gaza strip to replace that of Israel and Egypt, noting that neither was sovereign or had any designs to annex the territory. By that time the strip had become overcrowded with refugees, and a United Nations administration could be "meant to be a constructive compromise" to protect the inhabitants as well as Egyptian and Israeli interests.[16] That, however, was not to be. As the External Affairs minister noted in his memoirs: "I tried to get the Israelis out of the Gaza strip and succeeded by a United Nations administration. I had hoped that the strip could become a United Nations enclave for the refugees, but that was not possible. Egyptian civilian officials moved in immediately after the Israelis got out, although no Egyptian troops came with them. I do wish it had been possible."[17] Regardless of its theoretical and international legal intent, such a plan could hardly have been implemented given the vagaries of Middle Eastern politics.

Following the election of the Diefenbaker-led Progressive Conservatives in June 1957, there was no appreciable difference between government and opposition on the Palestinian refugee issue. Some three weeks after winning a Commons seat in a by-election, the new Secretary of State for External Affairs, Sidney E. Smith, gave a review of "Aspects of Canadian Foreign Policy" in the Commons.[18] Referring to the Palestinian refugees, Smith voiced concern for them and noted that an additional one half million dollars for the 1958 calendar year would be requested from Parliament. That was supplemented by the minister's announcement in the Commons on 23 January 1958, in response to the Secretary General's appeal that an additional $1 million worth of Canadian flour – 20,000 tons or a million bushels of Canadian wheat – could be made available. Spokespeople for the three opposition parties concurred, although Pearson, now in opposition, wanted to know "how much repatriation and resettlement has taken place among the refugees during the past 12 months."[19] "Very little," was Smith's response.[20] The following day, however, the minister stated: "If the financial situation of the agency develops as forecast, all the money which UNRWA will save as the result of our donations of flour will make possible an equivalent expenditure on rehabilitation projects."[21]

The decade evinced Canada's continued financial and other material support for the Palestinian refugees under agency auspices. The only imaginative proposal of any political substance was Pearson's "Gaza enclave," which was doomed before it was uttered. The Liberals and their Conservative successors knew that Israel could not be pressured on the issue. Other antagonists and protagonists were non-supportive in resolving the issue from either the Jewish or Arab side of the Middle East refugee conundrum.

4 Arms and the Reluctant Middleman

Reluctance to supply armaments to Israel was a hallmark of Canadian policy in this first decade. Officially, the government maintained an embargo on arms supply to the Middle East, abiding by United Nations resolutions on the issue. On 24 January 1949, however, permission to export thirty-six chipmunk trainer aircraft to Egypt and ten link trainers to Palestine by the Zionist Organization of Canada along with 2,210 storage batteries for motor vehicles was granted with the proviso that the shipment not affect the truce.[1]

In the wake of the armistice agreements between Israel and her neighbours in 1949, the Security Council, of which Canada was then still a member, adopted a Canada- and France-sponsored draft resolution on 11 August. The resolution noted "that these agreements supersede the truce provided for in the Security Council resolutions" (1948 of 29 May, No. 50; and of 15 July 1948, No. 43 – Clause 2 of the resolution). Commenting on the Security Council meetings of 4 to 11 August on arms shipments, Abba Eban, Israel's representative to the United Nations, noted that "the neutral members [Canada, Norway, Argentina, and Cuba], while leaning towards continuation of the embargo, declared that the decision lay with the arms supplying powers."[2]

The 11 August Security Council resolution led Ottawa to acknowledge that the arms embargo had been effectively removed. General McNaughton had on 4 August expressed the "opinion that [it] is not necessary to impose upon the states concerned the restrictive conditions of the Security Council's truce" (of 29 May 1948).[3] Moreover, Israel had since the inauguration of diplomatic relations requested the purchase of Harvard- and Cornell-type training aircraft as well as De Haviland chipmunks. The memorandum noted that Israel was asking for more arms from the Canadian Commercial Corporation, which acted as agent for government departments, and Canadian Arsenals Limited, another Crown corporation dealing with such matters. Payments were made in u.s. dollars.[4]

Consul General Avraham Harman dealt with arms purchases among the first major tasks after his assumption of duties. The arms acquisition process entailed a request first to the Canadian Commercial Corporation, which was to check on availability, then to the National Defence Board concerning both availability and affordability in light of Canadian defence interests. Cabinet would then deal with defence and foreign policy questions and reach decisions (except in routine matters where External Affairs could grant approval on behalf of cabinet).[5]

On 2 March Harman wrote to John Holmes of External Affairs in Ottawa regarding the training planes Israel's supply mission had requested.[6] The consul general noted that Terry MacDermott had told him that arms supply was still under review, and the request of the previous October from the Canadian Commercial Corporation had received a qualified negative response. MacDermott had indicated that he would notify Harman of a more appropriate time to submit a request. As for the political ramifications, MP David Croll had been kept informed by his Liberal colleague Pearson on the matter, but had not been consulted. Croll was somewhat agitated and sought a favourable response from Pearson. Harman, however, cautioned that in such matters there should be little publicity, for that was certainly not needed.[7]

Israel's difficulty in acquiring arms from a superpower like the United States necessitated a search in states such as Canada, France, the Scandinavian, or Latin American countries. Eban and Gideon Rafael of the Foreign Ministry also cautioned Sharett that although the United States was an "irreplaceable asset," arms acquisition from it was difficult without creating enormous political fuss and clashing with the United States State and Defence departments. They recommended, as had Harman, that (1) a public arms campaign be toned down; (2) test cases be avoided; (3) the United States be enlisted as an influence on Arabs for peace and not as an arms receiver; and (4) early realistic peace treaties from Arabs be secured and the United Kingdom be restrained "from running amok."[8]

The manifest hesitancy of the Canadian bureaucracy was evident in its communications during the winter of that year. General McNaughton had written to Eban that "the Canadian government decided that internal security and legitimate defence requirements should be the criteria governing the approval of any applications for permits to export arms."[9] Four days later, External Affairs' Arnold Heeney informed the minister that cabinet should not consent to quotation requests by Israel's supply mission since the Middle East was combustible and Israel continued to defy the General Assembly resolution on Jerusalem. He also noted that Israel "might conceivably embark on a policy of the continual influx of immigrants and economic pressures dictate it."[10] As a result, on 17 January cabinet agreed that it could not grant permission to export the $2 million in military equipment to Israel.[11]

On 23 February Harman expressed concern to MacDermott over the pace and size of weapons expansion in Egypt and Syria. The following day, R.G. Robertson of External Affairs notified Pearson that the policy was under review and "any revised list [to] be submitted will be given sympathetic consideration." The same was conveyed to Harman.[12] Subsequently, MacDermott outlined the principles on arms shipments as follows: (a) no discrimination between Israelis and Arabs; (b) government knowledge of all sizes and character of shipments going out; (c) shared information among Canada, the United Kingdom and the United States; (d) pressure on both the Arabs and the Israelis to curtail arms requirements and reach a settlement; (e) consideration of the strategic importance of this policy for the West.[13]

The External Affairs minister on 21 March submitted to cabinet a memorandum recommending the export to Israel of 100 Browning machine guns, eighteen anti-aircraft units, and approximately 18,000 rounds of anti-aircraft ammunition. On 28 April, a month after cabinet approval, Pearson informed Harman that certain arms shipments were approved which were not to be used for aggressive purposes or to obstruct implementation of United Nations resolutions on Palestine.[14]

As a consequence of cabinet approval, the Israel defence ministry was pleased at the breaking of the "ice."[15] Harman then noted, "I have, meanwhile, heard on fairly reliable authority that the peculiar 'understanding' referred to by Pearson in his original letter to us, approves the original list of arms requests we made was put in in order to cover the possibility that when this story leaks out, and I suppose it inevitably will, the Canadian government will be able to answer any attack made against it on the grounds that it has provided arms to a country which has not implemented United Nations resolutions. I interpret this as a further example of the histrionics of the government here to Catholic opinion on the Jerusalem question."[16]

During the summer, Heeney recommended that the minister deny Israel's request to buy Mosquito aircraft because he felt that Israel was too strong. He further noted that the request was not for routine equipment according to the British Foreign Office.[17] Cabinet, however, did on 16 August approve the sale of Mosquito replacement parts, and Pearson's 24 October request to export 200 Browning air-cooled machine guns to Israel.[18]

During the year A.R.L. McNaughton, General Andrew McNaughton's son, became Israel's accredited purchasing agent in Canada in the hope that such a respectable name would benefit Israel in the acquisition of arms.[19] In reporting to Comay, the consul general stated that machine guns and anti-aircraft shells were readily available.[20] Nevertheless, on 25 May Britain, France, and the United States issued the Tripartite Declaration, which included provisions for (1) the maintenance of forces for legitimate self-defence; (2) arms supplied on the understanding that they were not for aggression; (3) British, French, and u.s. action to prevent violations of frontiers or armistice lines. That declaration coupled with the British embargo caused some Israeli concern, but did not substantially affect the process of arms acquisition. At the end of May Harman reported that henceforth, applications would be considered in the light of those declared principles; namely, (1) assuring internal security; (2) use for non-aggressive purposes; (3) permitting sponsoring governments to play their part in the defence of the area as a whole. The latter disturbed Harman because he felt that essentially it gave the Arabs the upper hand.[21]

As a result of the outbreak of hostilities in Korea on 25 June and Canada's involvement with the United Nations action in repelling North Korea's aggression, the consul general remarked that Canada had been caught on one foot and that Israel could only place orders after Canadian production had intensified.[22] With reference to McNaughton's report to Israel's supply mission in New York, Harman informed Comay that there appeared to be goodwill on the part of the Canadian government in spite of London's embargo on Israel.[23]

No hard and fast rules were laid down in the following years, and each request was treated in light of current circumstances. Hence, there were various instances of approvals and disapprovals. While certain approvals of a minor nature were granted, others were denied in the first instance. These included such items as five 25-pounder guns and 25,000 rounds of ammunition denied on 22 May 1951.[24] Further requests followed by appeals elicited a more benign response from the External Affairs minister. After meeting with Croll, Pearson notified Heeney that "I think on general grounds that we should not be reluctant now to supply reasonable quantities of arms to Israel on the usual condition that they be used only for defence."[25] Although Heeney was known to be unenthusiastic about supporting Israel's arms requests, Pearson's stance was the significant factor. It found expression in one instance when Eban thanked him for his reception of Shimon Peres, then based with Israel's supply mission in New York, on the latter's visit to Ottawa in September of that year.

In 1952 there was greater co-ordination on the arms supply issue to Israel among Canada, the United Kingdom, and the United States. A 28 July memorandum dealing with confidential security information sent from the State department to the Canadian embassy in Washington noted that there was an informal agreement between Britain and the United States for a bi-monthly exchange of information on arms exports to Israel and the Arab states, including a list of arms approved for export.[26] Moreover, R.E. Collins of External Affairs' economic division noted previous consultations with the British Foreign Office and the u.s. State Department. As for current approval, he felt it would not be appropriate to consult the State Department because if the Foreign Office disapproved, then Canadian approval would not be granted. In a previous instance, External Affairs had gone ahead because the "order was too small to be disturbing."[27]

It was quite clear that the Canadian bureaucrats were being very wary, but the wariness was not always without cabinet support. Israel's Brigadier General A. Remez of the Ministry of Defence had asked Canadian industrialist Samuel Bronfman, who was also president of the Canadian Jewish Congress and a Liberal Party financial supporter, to use his influence with C.D. Howe, who held the twin portfolios of Trade and Commerce and Defence Production and was a major force within the St Laurent cabinet. Moreover, Remez sought to have the price of the 17-pounder cannons lowered. In what was described as an urgent situation, Remez hoped to get those items which were also destined to be sent to other North Atlantic Treaty Organization (NATO) countries.[28] Yosef Nevo, then Israeli consul general in Montreal, also called on Howe to win approval as Eban did with Pearson.[29] Notwithstanding considerable pressure and that Howe might have been amenable, the sale was not fulfilled.[30] The Canadian cabinet apparently considered it too risky.

It is of interest to note that one month later, there was a question of "balance" in arms payments between buyers. External Affairs' Dana Wilgress addressed a memorandum to the acting minister asking whether special permission granted to the Pakistanis for credit on wheat and arms was not a reversal of policy *vis-à-vis* Israel. He cited the Canada-Israel corporation which would not be used for the purchase of arms.[31] Balance did not seem to be the case although Pakistan was a member of the Commonwealth.

By 1953 it became cabinet policy to refuse the export of arms to Israel only because of technical difficulties or unavailability. A file note stated: "It is not the Government's policy to permit the export of military equipment to areas of unrest or possible conflict. Although Israel is technically at war with several of the Arab states, Cabinet decided that an exception was warranted in the case of Israel, as the country is rapidly becoming the one stable state in the Middle East and military supplies are required to maintain its security against internal and external pressures."[32]

The matter was also brought forward on 19 January, when Pearson received a joint United Zionist Council of Canada and Canadian Jewish Congress delegation who expressed concern over sales to the Arabs by the United Kingdom and the United States.[33] This was followed by a move to try and acquire the highly regarded F-86 Sabre jet fighter aircraft. On 17 February Josef Nevo reported to Sharett that since the Sabres were constructed in Canada under United States licence, U.S. permission was necessary. This led to Pearson's approaching U.S. Secretary of State John Foster Dulles. In addition, Brooke Claxton agreed and C.D. Howe had to be "tackled."[34] Eban and Croll were "ready [to] intervene when suitable."[35] On 4 March Eban called on the chairman of Canada's United Nations delegation about approaching the Canadian government for a small number of F-86s.[36] This was supplemented by a meeting between Israel's only Canadian-born cabinet minister, Dov Joseph, and Claxton in an "old boys" attempt, since both had been undergraduate students at McGill University.[37] No action, however, was taken.

On 17 March A.E. Ritchie of External Affairs noted for the undersecretary, "You might point out that while we have not always followed the lead of the United States and the United Kingdom in considering [the] export of military equipment to Israel (for example we recently approved the export of 200 tons of TNT to Israel over objections voiced both by the United States and the United Kingdom), we certainly have an obligation to take their views into account."[38]

The Canadian High Commissioner's office in London was also reluctant. In a secret memorandum addressed to the External Affairs' European division, R.E. Collins noted that "it would be contrary to established Canadian policy to authorize the export of $950,000 worth of 25-pounder ammunition to Israel at the present time."[39] While the United States and the United Kingdom never objected to the export of large quantities of .50 calibre ammunition, since that was "routine" for maintaining internal security, the present case, he said, was different. Neither power would export 24,000 rounds of 25-pounders because it appeared that it was "far in excess of the legitimate needs of Israel to maintain existing levels of defensive armament."[40] In view of the tension during the previous winter and the U.S. and U.K. opinion that Israel had been "primarily" responsible for the situation, Collins advised that it would be difficult for Canada to justify the export of weapons "classified as highly offensive" to Israel.[41] Moreover, Britain and the United States, powers in the tripartite declaration, had already intervened in the tense situation.

The stands of such allied super and major powers were clearly manifest on one side in the delineation of policy, while there was pressure from the other side, specifically Canadian Industries Limited (CIL), to fulfil Israel's order for the 24,000 rounds of the 25-pounders, although Collins had argued that CIL would not suffer a setback by being refused permission to fulfil the order.

Pearson was less reticent than his civil servants. On 13 July he notified the High Commissioner in London and the ambassador in Washington that unless the Americans and British raised strong objections, he would recommend authorization to the Canadian Commercial Corporation in light of a possible change in United Kingdom policy.[42] Apparently, A.E. Ritchie and others remained reluctant with a feeling that Israel was stockpiling. The matter was to be further pursued when Comay arrived in Ottawa as resident minister plenipotentiary in the late summer.

The sale of Browning .5 inch guns was raised in the Commons on 11 March by George Nowlan, the Nova Scotia Progressive Conservative member, regarding SUMAC Industries Limited.[43] Davie Fulton, Nowlan's British Columbia colleague, asked again on behalf of the absent Nowlan about the sale involving Crown companies in Halifax. C.D. Howe responded that SUMAC was Israel's purchasing company – in which A.R.L. McNaughton was involved – and had bought the reconditioned guns from Canadian Arsenals Limited. In an earlier request, the minister's parliamentary assistant had indicated that Israel objected to any "information being made public."[44] The minister noted that the guns had been sold at fair prices. Howe stated that guns sold for scrap are unusable and that the price received for the workable guns by the Crown Assets Disposable Corporation from SUMAC was for workable and not scrap. This again confirmed that most sales to Israel involving minor arms were concluded. Still for Israel the major concerns were the acquisition of the 25-pounders, the Sabres, the T-33 trainers, and spare parts.[45]

Three days after presenting his credentials, Comay met with Pearson and several members of External Affairs including Ritchie, MacCallum, and Wilson. They discussed the requests as well as other matters, including British policy.[46] Comay noted that Croll had met with Pearson in New York over Israel's desired purchases in Canada. Pearson wanted to be satisfied that the United Kingdom and the United States were also selling Israel arms, stating his support for

Israel to be in a position to defend itself against aggression. Mindful of Canada's obligation to its NATO partners, the necessity for consultation was voiced. While Britain, France, and the United States carried primary responsibility for Middle East security, Pearson seemed more concerned about the two anglophone powers. Since Israel was buying in the West, he felt that Canada also had a political as well as a commercial interest. Comay cited Pearson's outspoken comment that he did not see why "the Americans and the British should be taking us for a ride."[47] The minister did note that cabinet would probably endorse if Howe and Claxton agreed. Moreover, he stated that the distinction between defensive and offensive weapons was artificial.[48]

A subsequent meeting on 8 September included A.E. Ritchie, C.S. Ritchie, and Aviad Yafeh of the Israeli embassy. When asked about Israel's preference for Canadian equipment, Comay stated: (1) Canadian equipment was thought to be in better condition; (2) "Canadian policy regarding the different states in the Middle East does not fluctuate as much as that of the United Kingdom"; (3) that Israel's desire for some independence from British supply sources was coupled with its desire to spread arms purchases over a wider area – in case of war, the arms flow from the United Kingdom might cease while it might continue from Canada; (4) Israel's dollar revenue was as great as or greater than its sterling income. Hence Israel did not have a dollar problem and was not discouraged from spending more freely on arms in Canada as opposed to the United Kingdom.[49]

Optimism – including Pearson's – was premature, as pressures were building among the major powers in opposition to Israeli purchases. The Joint Intelligence Board of the Defence Research Board, Department of National Defence in Ottawa, did not accede to the Israeli requests. The Joint Intelligence Board director stressed the need for equilibrium between Israel and the Arab states and demurred unless Britain, France, and the United States felt that an increase in Israel's military strength "would not jeopardize the equilibrium in the area."[50]

The meetings of early October between Comay and Pearson gave clear indications that London and particularly Washington were holding clear sway over the Canadian decision makers. Reporting on his 1 October meeting with Pearson, Comay acknowledged that his earlier optimism had been misplaced. He not only felt that Canada did not have a free hand but "in fact did not want to have one."[51] While Canada did not have as direct a concern as Britain or the United States, Comay sensed a one-sided arms embargo. He remarked that the External Affairs minister was not his usual affable self, claiming that Canada had to "keep faith" with the United States. Comay believed that the U.S. appeared unfriendly and was in fact hostile in exercising its influence.[52]

Comay hinted after his 8 October meeting with the External Affairs minister that Canada "shared Israel's irritation with the restrictive policy being followed by the United States on the export of arms to Israel."[53] Pearson objected to that remark, and it appeared that Comay had touched a diplomatic raw nerve. In a secret communiqué, however, Pearson informed Comay that the matter was being given careful consideration but that Canada was not prepared to enter any obligation.[54]

Comay's cable of 11 October noted Pearson's explanation that Canada was in fact obliged to consult with the Americans and British, and that the United States was opposed to Canada's supplying "under present conditions." Hence, only 150 surplus tank spares from Levy Brothers Auto Parts of Weston (Toronto) were granted an export permit. Washington's pressure on Israel had to be worked out by Israelis with "DC" but Canada could not ignore American views on Middle East security.[55] Matters were certainly not helped when Israel's purchasing agent in New York accompanied Comay to a meeting with C.S.A. Ritchie; the latter felt that the agent was misleading.[56] In the interim, Egypt expressed a desire to purchase no fewer than sixty Canadian-built Sabres.[57]

American influence was certainly undiminished. On 3 November Pearson informed Comay that there was no change and no possibility that the 25-pounders could be sold then or even by the middle of the following year. The Canadian Commercial Corporation claimed that due to their supply position, they could not accept orders. As a sop to Israel, Canada withdrew its temporary suspension of export permits on M-4 tank parts.[58] C.S.A. Ritchie, acting as under-secretary, informed Comay that the government was still waiting for a letter promising not to resell any of its purchases.[59] That letter was finally provided by the Israeli ministry of defence authorizing Comay to make the commitment.[60] So Canadian arms supply policy toward Israel remained subject to British and especially U.S. constraints, limiting itself to "little purchases yes; big purchases no," a policy manifestly not in accord with the External Affairs minister's "freer hand."

American constraint was also due to the fact that in a number of instances Canadian military and other equipment which originated in the United States required its approval for resale. At the beginning of 1954 C.D. Howe had denied the export of tank tracks from the Levy Brothers to Israel.[61] In discussing this with Howe, Comay noted that the minister said that the United States was "absolutely adamant" in its refusal.[62] Howe suggested that the attempt should be made through the Israeli embassy in Washington and followed up by Israel's military attaché, who also served as attaché in Ottawa.[63] In a memorandum prepared by External Affairs' R.A. MacKay, the civil servant's reluctance manifested itself again. On 27 January he expressed the belief that Israel was more than equipped for defence and that there should be no export for offensive operations.[64]

The External Affairs minister was not pleased with the situation and wanted to know whether John Foster Dulles and Britain's Anthony Eden in their recent discussions on the Middle East had been holding out on Canada.[65] It appears that Pearson became more forceful and in fact resented Howe's recommendation to approach Washington. Meeting with Pearson on 7 March, Comay noted Pearson's claim that Howe's suggestion regarding the State Department was out of line. Although irked by the State Department, Pearson said that Israel was not at fault for approaching it. In future, he wanted to be consulted before any referral to Washington through the Israeli embassy there. Moreover, Pearson resented Howe's intrusion on a matter that was his department's concern.[66] The External Affairs minister had earlier expressed his annoyance with Howe when he lunched with Comay at Ottawa's Rideau Club on 2 March.[67] In his memoirs Pearson recalled that the sale of "defensive" equipment was not criticized since "it was agreed by the great majority in the House of Commons that an embargo on all arms shipments to either side would be unfair to Israel."[68]

Comay and Croll called on Pearson on 29 March and again on 9 April concerning the tank tracks. Once more MacKay expressed his doubt in a memorandum to the minister claiming that the tank tracks could expose Canada to criticism for disturbing the equilibrium of military power. A.E. Ritchie also stated that the commercial advantage to Canada would be outweighed by political and practical disadvantages.[69] Nevertheless, Pearson recommended to cabinet that Israel's request for the propellant charges for the 25-pounders be granted an export permit. The United Kingdom approved the sale, but the United States did not think it could be justified "for defensive purposes."[70]

Israel's military purchases began to focus on the F-86 Sabres. In view of previous enquiries, the acting minister had notified the ambassador in Washington and the High Commissioner in London that the United States had approved the sale of two dozen Sabres. The shift in the American position spurred the Israelis, and they were particularly concerned with ongoing American approval. For one thing, Canadair, the Canadian manufacturer, was a subsidiary of the U.S. North American Aviation Company, which was licensed to manufacture the Sabres. Comay called on Pearson on 17 June in a major effort to engage his support for a request to the American government. Israel was in need of state-of-the-art jet fighters of which the Canadian-built Sabre was highly regarded. The first negative U.S. response was conveyed to Comay on 8 July.[71]

Comay noted a nagging problem concerning External Affairs' Wilson of the economic division. Wilson's apparent distrust of Israel might have been a reflection of his superiors' attitudes.[72] Israel kept close watch on London and Washington for a change of mind.[73]

In the interim, Pearson sent a memo to cabinet for approval of $964,071 worth of M4 tank parts and tracks, "deliverance to be spread as evenly as possible over a six month period so as not to arouse Arab anxieties." He recommended deferral of the Sherman tank tracks because the $224 thousand price would be over the amount "reckoned safe by the State department."[74] Cabinet approval was again sought on 17 September for the 25-pounder sale, which came a month after Jules Léger, then under-secretary, sought to find out whether the United Kingdom had informed Canada of their 25-pounder sale to Israel.[75]

Since Britain had lifted its arms supply embargo, Comay met with Pearson, who was rather depressed both that the embargo lift included Egypt and at Washington's apparent new sympathy toward the Arab states.[76] This seemed to hasten the 25-pounder approval with the proviso, "if Canadian supply considerations make it possible to release the equipment requested"[77] although Pearson admitted that the sale was influenced "to some extent" by the United Kingdom sale to Israel.[78] By the year's end, Léger noted that there had been embarrassment over sales, and because of the divergent policies of the United Kingdom, the United States, and France – not to mention U.S. pressure.[79]

Colonel Nasser's assumption of full power in 1954 and Egypt's assertion of a greater international role, as witnessed in the Bandung conference of April 1955, seemed to make it a significant player in the Third World. The Arab-Israeli, or more specifically the Egyptian-Israeli, conflict came into sharper focus as an impending tempest loomed over the Mediterranean. It was further exacerbated by Egypt's agreement with the Soviet bloc on a major acquisition of arms in September. Egypt's reliance on Western arms was over. Israel now strove to keep some semblance of balance with its hesitant suppliers. As the reluctant middleman, Canada was now becoming more involved, receiving further Israeli requests on the one hand, and checking with London and Washington on the other. Israel was pressing.

Earlier, on 13 January, Comay had requested 500 more Browning machine guns and asked the External Affairs minister, "I would be grateful if your own sympathetic understanding of Israel's needs could be engaged in this request."[80] At the same time Elizabeth MacCallum, now chargé d'affaires at the new mission in Beirut, reported that Major-General E.L.M. Burns, Canadian head of the United Nations Truce Supervision Organization (UNTSO), was negative on the sale of arms.[81] A.E. Ritchie subsequently noted in an internal memorandum that neither arms nor ammunition had been sold to Jordan, Lebanon, and Syria between 1950 and 1954, nor to Egypt, Iran and a negligible amount to Iraq and Saudi Arabia.[82] According to the London High Commissioner's communication to the minister in Ottawa, the British supplied arms to Egypt to keep Nasser "sweet."[83]

According to Israel's officials, George Kidd felt that Israel was militarily strong, and his feelings appeared as a restraining influence on Ottawa.[84] Comay again met with Pearson on 6 June, and as a result Léger prepared a memorandum for the minister's presentation to cabinet on 22 July recommending the supply of 600 additional Brownings of .30 calibre, "to be delivered at 200 per annum starting April 1956."[85]

The Soviet bloc (Czechoslovakian)-Egyptian arms deal intensified Israel's purchasing efforts as External Affairs feared Israel would counter with further requests from western sources.[86] George Kidd kept reporting on the mood in Israel and on the rumoured delivery of French Mystère jets.[87] It appeared that France might be emerging as a stable source of supply for Israel. At the same time, Comay's repeated requests to External Affairs' R.A.D. Ford and Léger consisted of what was regarded as a defensive and offensive mix. Again A.E. Ritchie noted for the under-secretary the matter of consulting with the British and Americans on the sales: "We do not actually seek their approval, but we ask if they would be prepared to release shipments if the requests were directed to them."[88] That seemed to be a subtler form of acknowledging influence rather than overt pressure. Léger did inform Pearson on 1 December on the matter of arms to Israel, and that there had been no increase in requests resulting from the Soviet bloc-Egyptian arms deal. Nevertheless, there would be a problem were Canada asked for the Sabres.[89]

As Pearson's planned visit to Asia, with a scheduled call on Nasser, approached, Comay extended an invitation for him to visit Israel. The Israeli ambassador had again expressed his concern that the Egyptian army would be equipped with Soviet and Czech weapons, and asked how Israel should react as the military balance turned against it.[90] Such concern was also expressed earlier in a joint United Zionist Council of Canada-Canadian Jewish Congress submission to the External Affairs minister on 19 September, as well as an appeal on 29 November to the prime minister by Claude Jodoin, president of the Trades and Labour Congress of Canada and Donald MacDonald, secretary of the Canadian Congress of Labour. The labour leaders noted that the one-sided arms embargo *vis-à-vis* Israel, veiled as "nonintervention," resulted in the tragic example of Spain during the civil war when the Allied powers did not supply the Loyalists in their struggle with Franco's forces.[91] That had been preceded by Comay's 2 November meeting with Léger and Ford, in which they had reviewed events since the Soviet bloc-Egyptian arms deal and stressed the need for requested military supplies from Canada.[92]

Pearson's visit with President Nasser in Cairo on the evening of 10 November mostly revolved on the arms issue. Nasser claimed to have called the American and British "bluff" in securing arms from behind the Iron Curtain.[93] While trying to assure the Egyptian president that Britain and the United States were considerably less prejudiced and partial than he thought, Pearson stated: "We knew from our own experience in Canada that Israeli requests for arms which would add to their present level of offensive strength were turned down in the three capitals, in spite of great pressure exercised on their behalf. That pressure would now be much greater and more difficult to resist. But where would an arms race get us?"[94] Nasser and Pearson agreed that Foreign Minister Sharett was a moderate in terms of seeking a peace settlement, yet Pearson concluded: "I confess that my talk did not give me any reason for undue optimism that a solution would be found in the immediate future."[95]

Since Pearson did not stop in Israel during his visit because a Sabbath (Saturday) meeting was taboo in the Jewish state, a meeting was arranged with him and Sharett during the latter's visit to Ottawa on 1 December. Comay and Ford attended, and Pearson reported on his meeting with Nasser and discussed the general situation.[96] Pearson promised to study the possibility of anti-aircraft, anti-tank and machine gun purchases and keep in touch with Comay.[97] On the other hand, according to an External Affairs note on the same meeting, Pearson agreed to immediately approve the pending Israeli requests.[98] Moreover, R.M. MacDonnell, writing Comay on behalf of the under-secretary on 2 December, informed him that some arms were being released.[99]

Comay and Pearson met again with Ford on 23 December. Reviewing the situation Pearson remarked that the 40 mm anti-aircraft guns were unavailable but would check again when available. The hoary question of "defensive weapons" re-emerged in the other requests including radar and aircraft. As for Washington and the matter of arms supply, Comay suggested that Canada be given the business if the same conditions were available. Pearson agreed and asked Ford why Canada should not be in the picture. The minister felt that since the Americans complained that they had to know what the Canadians were doing, why should the Canadians not know what the Americans were doing?[100]

Canada's sales of some Harvard training aircraft to Egypt and especially the saga of the F-86 interceptor jets sale to Israel was to dominate the Canadian-Israeli diplomatic scene in the following year.

5 Bureaucratic Dispositions

Political events and bureaucratic activity were leading to the fateful year of 1956. Joint submissions to the government by the Canadian Jewish Congress and the United Zionist Council of Canada stressed Israel's position on Arab arms acquisitions as well as other matters related to the Arab-Israeli conflict, including Iraqi Jews and German reparations.[1] Israeli confrontation with Syria over Lake Hulah and El Hama as well as Israel's right of free passage through the Suez Canal were causing concern.

Canadian political and civil servants retained their cautious approach during 1952, as Israel continued to seek support for direct negotiations with the Arabs. In one instance, Eban solicited support from Canadian United Nations delegates D.M. Johnson and Elizabeth MacCallum to sponsor a resolution of such a nature. But External Affairs objected, noting: "A good case is made against sponsoring any resolution of the kind indicated,"[2] and MacCallum later stated: "Present draft would not do as a draft sponsored by neutral states."[3] As in the past, MacCallum's less than positive attitude toward Israel somewhat chagrined Eban. His communication to Pearson stated his belief in the necessity for a clear statement by the United Nations on the need for free negotiations among sovereign states: "I was under the assumption, based on a knowledge of past Canadian policies, that Canada would have no difficulty in accepting it, and it was in that spirit that I took the liberty of suggesting the attendance of the Canadian representative at the meeting ... May I therefore suggest that she [MacCallum] await a chance of speaking with me before influencing this draft in any substantive way."[4] Eban's letter surprised Johnson who took umbrage and defended MacCallum.[5]

An External Affairs major expert on the Middle East and known to all for her pro-Arab leanings, MacCallum felt it necessary to see that both sides of the argument were presented. She always regarded Israel as Pearson's "blind spot."[6] Nevertheless, MacCallum always retained the mandarins' respect.

Israel's desire for Canadian support for the "free and untrammelled negotiations" had not won over the bureaucrats of the failed 18 December 1952 General Assembly resolution; although the delegation did finally support the direct negotiations principle. Israel's appreciation of the support was explicitly conveyed to Pearson by Sharett and Eban in the wake of the General Assembly's consideration.[7] Pearson's concern over a neutral position was a not insignificant factor in Canada's involvement in committee and the plenum.

Toward the end of January, there was increased concern over growing antisemitism in the Soviet bloc, with the arrest of six Jewish doctors in Russia and the purges in Czechoslovakia. Pearson responded to Croll's request with a statement in the Commons on 15 January. Stressing the terrible developments, the minister said that External Affairs had not had sufficient time "to make possible a balanced assessment of its probable implications. That it may prove to be a very serious matter indeed is, I think, obvious to all of us."[8] The issue was again impressed upon Pearson when on 19 January, he met with a joint United Zionist Council of Canada-Canadian Jewish Congress delegation on Soviet antisemitism and the sale of arms and jets to Egypt by the United Kingdom. Pearson reportedly showed sympathy and understanding, "and promised to do what might be possible within the framework of existing Canadian policy."[9]

Yosef Nevo, Israeli consul general in Montreal, reported on the matter of Soviet antisemitism and in particular the forthcoming General Assembly, noting that Canada was concerned, and the minister was approaching the matter with great caution. Pearson hoped that Israel would not introduce the matter on the United Nations agenda, believing that a long drawn-out debate might harm the Jews. Castigating Soviet antisemitism could play into the Soviet game *vis-à-vis* the Arabs and result in an increase in East-West tensions. Moreover, Pearson felt that it could lead into despondency in the Jewish world.[10] Gideon Rafael of the Israeli delegation seemingly agreed and opted to broach the subject using the Polish and Czech items on the agenda.[11]

Increased tensions from Arab infiltration and subsequent Israeli reprisal raids finally reached a peak on 14 and 15 October, when Israel raided the Jordanian village of Qibiya. Two days later the Tripartite

Declaration powers referred the matter to the Security Council, which resulted in Israel's being censured in a resolution on 24 November. Prior to that the obvious lack of balance resulted in the Jewish-Canadian leadership issuing a statement on 26 October objecting to the condemnation of reprisals and the ongoing guerrilla warfare against Israel.[12]

Security Council censure of Israel elicited an exceptionally forthright response from John Holmes of External Affairs. In a memorandum to the European division on the charges against Israel he singled out the British for their lack of objectivity: "The pro-Arab bias is so deep-rooted in the Foreign Office and the Conservative party, with the honourable exception of the Prime Minister, that it has never been possible for them to look at the Arab-Israel questions fairly. This bias is constantly fed no doubt by reports from Glubb[13] and his associates in Amman, whose bland ignoring of the facts of Arab-Jewish relations in Palestine during the past decade or so must be heard to be believed. This bias is also fed by the British press, in which the Israeli point of view is practically never mentioned ... It now appears that everyone from the Archbishop of York down is enjoying another orgy of Israelophobia." Criticizing u.s. lack of objectivity, he continued, "I wish that we could somehow use our influence to secure a resolution which would cry 'a plague on both your houses,' and not encourage one side by denouncing the other."[14] He added that it would be unfair to Israel, ignoring entirely – save for some reports – previous Arab activities.[15] Such emphatic comment was indeed a rarity among the bureaucrats.

Following an attack on a bus at the Scorpion Pass in which eleven Israelis were killed, Comay on 24 March 1954 met with J.A. Chapdelaine of External Affairs giving Israel's account of the attack. Then on 9 April Comay met with Pearson to stress the importance of direct negotiations and the need to stop the murderous attacks as witnessed in the bus tragedy. When Pearson expressed his understanding of Israel's distress and sense of persecution but demurred from reprisals, Comay pointed out that reprisals were appropriate because Arabs only understood when being hit back. The notion of a United Nations force was broached during the meeting.[16] Comay had also reported that he had had contacts with the ccf in maintaining their support.[17] Yet, pro-Arab sentiment was not unnoticed in the bureaucracy. Kenneth Kirkwood, the former Canadian High Commissioner in Pakistan, filed a report about his recent tour of some Arab countries in which his Arab sympathy was obvious.[18]

While discussions of attacks and reprisals continued in the Security Council, there was no amelioration of the situation. Additional officers, including Canadians, were added to upgrade the United Nations Truce

Supervision Organization in an effort to appease the conflicting parties. In particular, Major-General E.L.M. Burns of Canada was chosen to succeed General V. Bennike. On another matter, the day before he was officially upgraded to ambassador, Comay communicated with External Affairs legal advisor, Max Wershof, on the subject of a Canada-Israel extradition treaty.[19]

On 8 September the Israeli ambassador again called on Pearson regarding Israel's situation. The minister understood – apparently from British assessments – that Israel had more arms than her four Arab neighbours. Pearson wanted either confirmation or correction of that impression before taking further action. Comay tried to convince him of the seriousness of the situation regarding the Suez agreement and American attempts to assure Egypt and Iraq and wanted him to try and guide American thinking. It was agreed that the two would keep in touch with each other while the minister was at the General Assembly "and regard myself [Comay] as an 'unofficial member' of his delegation."[20] This was again emphasized by Samuel Bronfman and Edward Gelber of the Canadian Jewish Congress and United Zionist Council respectively in a joint memorandum to Pearson on behalf of Canadian Jewry. They expressed concern over the increased British and American military aid to the Arab states, and asked the minister to use his influence on the two powers.[21]

In the autumn, Israel attempted to sail one of its ships – the *Bat Galim*, bound for Haifa – through the Suez Canal. The Egyptians seized the ship for alleged violation of the Constantinople Convention of 1888 and the Security Council resolution of 1 September 1951. Aviad Yafeh of Israel's Ottawa embassy called at the External Affairs European division, explaining that the sending of the *Bat Galim* through the canal was an intentional test case. In a memorandum on the meeting, John Holmes added a note indicating what he regarded as fair and objective: "I have never been able to understand why there was anything *sinister* about the Israeli motive in putting up a test case in the Suez Canal, even if this was deliberately intended to draw attention away from the border incidents. It is high time that Israeli violations of the armistice were seen in perspective, and that the Arabs were not allowed to get away with the argument that they are the righteous ones who stand by the decisions of the United Nations."[22] Holmes' unequivocal attitude was certainly unique among the denizens of External Affairs.

Under-Secretary Léger expressed his sympathy regarding the *Bat Galim* and the Israeli spy trials in Alexandria at a meeting with the Israeli ambassador. Comay claimed that the trials resembled the Soviet

Jewish doctors sham plot. Australia, Scandinavia, South Africa, and the United States tried to get the ship released.[23] Regarding that meeting Ford noted in a memorandum for the under-secretary: "In particular, I believe that the future of our diplomatic mission in Egypt should not be jeopardized at this early stage by pressing too vigorously Israeli contentions which may not be as well founded as Israeli spokesmen make them appear."[24] While Comay's *démarche* was designed to seek Canadian pressure on Egypt, Ford recommended caution. As for the *Bat Galim*, it was deemed advisable that Canada should continue to consult with the United Kingdom, the United States, and perhaps France. No action was to be taken concerning the spy trials beyond consultations with the Americans and British. Ford further recommended that such be conveyed diplomatically to Comay.[25] For some civil servants, political pitfalls were to be judiciously avoided.

With the expansion of External Affairs Middle East section, MacCallum went off to Beirut as chargé d'affaires, initiating Canada's diplomatic relations with Lebanon. Yet the bureaucracy was still reluctant *vis-à-vis* Israel. Yafeh tried to get Canada's National Defence College to visit Israel but was unsuccessful. The overly cautious preferred non-involvement, possibly due both to Canada's connection with the United Nations Truce Supervision Organization and to its sensitivity over arms purchases. Moreover, there was the impression of Canadian ambassador MacDermott, during his February-March visit, as well as Chargé d'Affaires Kidd's assessments that Israel was too strong.[26] MacDermott was concerned about the Palestinian refugees regardless of who did what to them. He also left the impression that he regarded world Jewry's financial aid as not so much an expression of Jewish solidarity as a love of the West for Israel: as he remarked, they are "all Americans and Canadians."[27]

On 30 March Comay and Pearson met to discuss Israel's concern over the clashes with Egypt.[28] Pearson was not enthusiastic about the Turco-Iraq (Baghdad or Central Treaty Organization – CENTO) pact which had been signed in February. The pact was part of a so-called "northern tier," which was joined by Britain, Pakistan, and Iran, a buffer between Moslem states and the Soviet Union. Turkey was also a member of the North Atlantic Treaty.

In his memoirs, Pearson noted his lack of enthusiasm and oblique criticism of Dulles and the Baghdad pact: "Pushed by Dulles in his passion for surrounding the communist bloc with a ring of mini NATOS. Nasser considered this pact a threat to his ambitions to unify and lead all the Arab states, especially because of the inclusion of Iraq in the new arrangement."[29] Nasser was aiming to get Soviet assistance and hoped for Western assistance as well, "particularly from that champion of nationalism against imperialism, John Foster Dulles. It did not work out that way."[30]

In his communication of 31 March to Arthur Lourie, Comay stated that he felt that Israel had failed to turn American policy away from seeking alliances with the Arabs in the absence of an Arab-Israel settlement. He continued: "The lines we can most effectively argue at present to interested governments is that if the 'northern tier' arrangements and the attempts to get as many Arab states as possible to go along with them, are to proceed anyway, the prejudice to us can be remedied by the parallel measures we are seeking. Unless I am instructed to the contrary, that will be where the emphasis will lie in any talks here, although I will naturally express as well our fundamental objection to the whole business."[31] The same day Comay reported to the Commonwealth division of Israel's Foreign Office that he was keeping up his contacts with Liberal parliamentarians Leon Crestohl and David Croll, and he did not think that a Canadian Jewish Congress-United Zionist Council of Canada deputation to Pearson was advisable at that time. Comay also noted that the Egyptian embassy was then distributing an anti-Israel pamphlet.[32]

In his reply to Comay Lourie pointed out Sharett's concern over Western strategies for defence and Arab partnership as potentially explosive: "Our efforts in this circumstances continue to be directed to seeking parallel arrangements by way of arms and direct security guarantees. At one point we seemed to have made some progress in Washington. Today, I am not so sure and presumably Eban's next talk with Dulles will tell the tale."[33]

Two weeks later Comay wrote to Pearson requesting a review of matters and to discuss issues in and around Israel. On 2 May he met with Ford and reported that Israel's notions seemed to have had an impact on departmental thinking that regional pacts would be built on sand until there was a resolution of the Arab-Israel dispute. It seemed to him that the Arabs "had complained of feeling neglected and isolated while Israel's strength was built up, but now the roles seemed to be reversed."[34] Comay had the feeling that Canada wanted credit for some initiative away from the attacks upon Israel. Certainly Israel wanted Canada to employ its influence in Washington and London. As far as the border situation was concerned, External Affairs felt that Israel had erred in not accepting Burns' Gaza proposals[35] that Egypt and Israel accept joint Egyptian-Israeli patrols, local commander agreements, barbed-wire obstacles along certain portions of the demarcation line, and outposts and patrols to be staffed by regular Egyptian and Israeli troops only.[36]

As the summer wore on, the situation between Israel and its neighbours continued to deteriorate. Pearson received a joint delegation from the Canadian Jewish Congress and the United Zionist Council of Canada as well as a written submission in September. The submission called for (1) Canada to adopt a position that frontier redefinition should not mean ceding of territory; (2) no arms shipments to the Arabs until peace was achieved; (3) Canadian support of the Dulles proposal for an international loan to help finance the resettlement of Palestinian refugees in Arab lands; (4) encouraging Arab states to resume normal economic relations with Israel; (5) supporting Israel in challenging the Egyptian blockade of the Suez Canal and the Gulf of Aqaba; (6) Canadian offering of its experience of interstate management of river waters with particular reference to the Johnston plan; (7) advocacy of the recognition of Israel by the Arab states.[37] The submission remained just that.

At his meeting on 2 November with Léger and Ford, Comay reviewed recent events starting with the Czechoslovakian (Soviet bloc)-Egyptian arms deal and its implications for the West with the present Soviet drive into the Middle East which would turn the flank of the North Atlantic treaty, leapfrog the "northern tier," rally anti-Western tendencies, and give a base for communist penetration south and into Africa. The ambassador pointed out that Israel and Turkey were the only two states in the region which were relatively free from internal weakness and anti-Western sentiment. He attacked the thesis that the West's difficulties were caused by Israel's emergence and pointed out that difficulties were inevitable and similar to those elsewhere. What mattered, he said, in a possible four-power declaration to which Israel was not opposed was the practical implication of whether the Arabs would go on getting arms or not. It appeared that Nasser was riding a crest and getting the best of both worlds, but should be cut off from Western aid as long as he pursued his present course. He explained Israel's requirements and pointed out that it was trying to avoid war while wanting a security alliance with the United States covering arms supplies and treaty guarantees, Israel would vigorously act to defend its sea and air communications, water resources and vital interests in the Gulf of Aqaba, Nitzan, Birot, etc.[38]

In the same report, Comay noted that Coldwell, Diefenbaker, and Social Credit leader Solon Low had commented on the fact that Pearson was stopping off in Cairo without visiting Israel. Again, extending his invitation to Pearson to talk with Sharett in Israel, he told Ford that it would be an unhappy impression in such tense circumstances for so eminent a friend as Pearson to pass within a few miles of Israel on a courtesy visit to Cairo. Pearson, however, subsequently attempted to justify his Israeli non-stop in his address to the Commons on 24 January 1956. He noted that two cabinet ministers, two senators, and six parliamentarians had visited Israel in 1955, including two party leaders and Diefenbaker himself – who was still not his party's leader: "I am flabbergasted by the suggestion that all of these visits by such distinguished Canadians were more than equalled by a day and a half stopover by me in Cairo on the way home from a Colombo plan meeting."[39]

Nevertheless, Pearson's meeting in Cairo with the Egyptian president still meant a need to meet with his Israeli counterpart or perhaps someone higher within the very near future. On 1 December Comay and Ford met in Ottawa for an hour and a quarter. Discussions focused on Pearson's talks with Nasser and Foreign Minister Mahmoud Fawzi who was described as inconsequential for he "was clearly not a policy maker."[40] Reviewing his talk with Nasser, Pearson also asked about the prospect of territorial settlement and whether Israel could make concessions in the Negev: that would have entailed sacrifices such as the right of way while retaining sovereignty. According to Sharett such measures would be feasible if peace and the use of Haifa port by Jordan were possible. If the Soviets could win by short wars, they would not be conciliatory.[41] Sharett also met the same day with Prime Minister St Laurent, with whom he discussed Britain's Anthony Eden's offer of mediation, and Governor-General Vincent Massey.

The passage through the Negev was raised again in Comay's 23 December meeting with Pearson and Ford. It was pointed out that in spite of understandings reached between the late King Abdullah of Jordan – who had been assassinated in 1951 – and Israel, no action had been taken.[42] As far as a peace program was concerned, the minister was "not thoroughly convinced."[43]

External Affairs personnel exemplified the ethos of prudent approaches to issues which is not an unusual hallmark of a democracy's civil service. In Canada's case, it is interesting to note that the minister was himself a former bureaucrat whose political approach at times belied his former background. Still, his actions and the stands he took in 1956 and 1957 displayed a keen sense of political timing in the case of the Sabres and in the events involved in the Sinai-Suez affair.

6 The Saga of the Unsheathed Sabres

A strictly neutral state need not face a dilemma in supplying arms to states at war or in conflict. Others, however, might face a quandary when asked for arms by warring states with whom they have normal relations. Such a state may be guided by the principle of selling weapons only for defensive purposes and supplying them in moderation after meticulous bureaucratic, executive, and legislative consideration, enabling it to maintain a kind of equilibrium with the conflicting states. Trying to maintain a balance between the antagonists is onerous, especially when an external factor – in this case an unfriendly superpower – creates a massive disequilibrium which is neither offset nor matched by the other superpower or its allies.

Canada again faced such a dilemma in dealing with Israel's request to purchase a squadron of twenty-four Canadian-manufactured F-86 Sabre jet aircraft interceptors. The saga of the diplomatic and political process during 1956, involving the decision first to sell and then to suspend sale at the outbreak of the Sinai-Suez campaign, reveals a significant aspect of the Canadian government's diplomacy of prudence during the first decade of its relations with Israel.

Some sagas have romantic heroes and swashbucklers ever ready to unsheathe their weapons, others have staid and sober characters. On the executive side of this narrative, the principle personalities were the Liberal Prime Minister St Laurent and in particular the External Affairs Minister Pearson, who worked well with St Laurent's reluctance in deciding to release the Sabres. The domestic bureaucrats and international public servants tended toward greater political neutrality.

The Opposition professed commitment to the survival of one of the states in conflict especially when the inventory of military hardware had been completely offset between the adversaries. The press was not a major factor in the process, although a number of the more influential dailies supported the Sabres sale. The monolithic Zionist-dominated Jewish-Canadian community had no effect of a discernible nature.

Among the non-Canadian actors were the Israeli ambassador, the United States government in the person of its Secretary of State, the British and French governments, and to a much lesser degree the NATO partners. Finally, Egypt and the other Arab states had a diminished effect on the Canadian government after it had become the predominant "unequalizer" with Soviet bloc support.

Israeli interest in the Sabres took a more serious turn early in 1956 as pressure mounted for the purchase. The problem increased when it was revealed that the government had sold a number of Harvard aircraft trainers to Egypt. The resulting embarrassment was aggravated by the inept manner in which cabinet members responded.

The Opposition's querulous assault intensified when the government mishandled its enquiries. The major actors during the January and February sittings of Parliament were the Progressive Conservative Party – particularly John Diefenbaker, the leading pro-Israel figure in his party – leader George Drew, Donald Fleming, George Pearkes, and Douglas Harkness. Pro-labour Zionist Alistair Stewart, leader M.J. Coldwell, Colin Cameron, and Stanley Knowles acted for the CCF.

Government fumbling can best be shown in the following incidents. Stewart began by asking about the Harvards shipment, to which Pearson claimed he knew "of no shipments of Canadian aircraft to Egypt or any orders for such shipments."[1] The Minister of National Defence, Ralph Campney, then said that he had no knowledge of military equipment destined for Egypt. Stewart asked about gun mountings on the planes, to which Pearson responded, "I do not know how you can put a gun mounting on a Harvard training aircraft."[2] He got his answer when newspapers within hours published Department of National Defence photographs of Harvards firing machine guns and rockets and carrying bombs.[3] As to be expected, Stewart severely criticized the government in his major address on 18 January.

The Opposition's barrage was sustained by the Progressive Conservatives particularly over the shipments to Egypt. To catch its parliamentary breath from its ill-prepared question and answer confrontation, the government invoked a temporary embargo on arms shipments to the Middle East.[4] Now it was incumbent on the Liberals to respond and attempt to give a semblance of coherence to its hodge-podge approach to "Arms and the Middle East."

Pearson's 24 January statement was designed "to discuss first the question of the export of military equipment to the Middle East and secondly ... the political situation in that part of the world, with particular reference to the relations between Israel and her Arab neighbours."[5] The minister stated that the Egyptian request for fifteen Harvards had been received the previous June and approved on 7 July. Three of the Harvards had been shipped on 16 January, authorized by September's export permit. Disclaiming charges of disinformation, Pearson explained that the controls and checks system were based on the Export and Imports Permits Act of 1954, and that export permits could only be issued under the authority of the Minister of Trade and Commerce.

Pearson then outlined six points which governed policy under the act for military and cognate hardware: (1) for North Atlantic Treaty Organization and Commonwealth countries, no restrictions save for domestic requirements and security; (2) nothing for the Sino-Soviet bloc; (3) shipments to other areas after cabinet approval, with special care for "sensitive areas"; (4) shipments only to defence departments or a country's military establishment; (5) no shipment if it exceeds legitimate defence requirements or poses a threat to neighbouring countries; (6) no shipment if that "might increase any temptation to commit an aggression or begin a preventive war"[6] (which would include countries which would pose a threat to Canadian security or where the United Nations had declared an embargo).

Supplying Israel to the exclusion of the Arab states would have been considered unfriendly because of normal Arab diplomatic relations with Canada. Hence the government's control policy was guided by the American, British, and French tripartite declaration of 25 May 1950.[7] (Cabinet was then considering another Israeli request for 1,754 rounds for 25-pounder guns.) In sensitive areas, the Trade and Commerce minister acted only after agreements had been reached with National Defence and External Affairs and forwarded to cabinet. Treasury Board – a cabinet committee – subsequently had to approve, which could even result in full cabinet consideration.[8]

Pearson recalled that during the spring of 1955 suppliers enquired about Egyptian requests for Harvards and Sabres. The government was negative on the Sabres despite the commercial attractiveness: however, National Defence raised no objection to selling Harvards to friendly governments. As that was neither a policy issue nor an international consideration, Trade and Commerce received Pearson's approval. The export permit was issued in the first week of September, with the clear understanding that the planes would not be converted to combat aircraft.

Pearson denied that great quantities of modern Canadian arms were "flowing" to the region. To add some cogency to his case, the minister presented the 1954 military aid figures: $735,574.50 for Israel, $296.00 for Egypt, and nothing for the other Arab states. The 1955 amounts were $1,332,110.59 for Israel, $770,825.00 for Egypt, and a total of $70.0 for the other Arab states. The Egyptian figure was almost entirely for the fifteen Harvards. Israel's orders included 75 mm shells; anti-tank equipment; tracks and spare parts for World War II type tanks (Shermans); 25 pounder guns and accessories; .303 calibre Browning machine guns; 3- to 7-inch anti-aircraft guns, accessories, spare parts and ammunition (the largest portion of the total). There were also some Harvard parts for an unspecified recipient, but they were negligible.[9] There were official assurances of non-exportation, and the minister contended that the procedures were an effective control method. The government had been "handling this matter carefully and with a sense of international responsibility."[10]

Reviewing the situation Pearson first affirmed the need for Arab states to recognize the legitimate and permanent existence of the State of Israel in order to remove Israel's fear for its existence. Second, Israel had to pay compensation to the Arab refugees and contribute to a resettlement operation. Third, it was necessary to settle boundary disputes and produce permanent borders.[11]

Commenting on the Commons debate, the Israeli ambassador reported on the government's fumbling but was pleased with the pro-Israeli statements and with Pearson's "favourable" speech.[12] Comay had been disturbed earlier over PC and CCF support for the embargo. Conscious of traditional pacifism in certain CCF quarters, he had met with their caucus as well as with the PC and Social Credit members.[13]

Comay wrote to Pearson expressing Israel's concern over the expense and inconvenience of the temporary embargo and requesting a meeting prior to the Ottawa visit by United Kingdom Prime Minister Anthony Eden and Foreign Secretary Selwyn Lloyd.[14] The arms embargo was lifted on 2 February, and the next day the prime minister informed the Commons that there would be no interference with sending the remaining twelve Harvards to Egypt.[15]

In subsequent communications and meetings with Pearson, Comay conveyed Foreign Minister Sharett's written exchanges with U.S. Secretary of State Dulles. They expressed concern for Israel's vulnerability with the continuing Soviet weaponry supply to Egypt. The 1950 tripartite declaration was neither a sufficient deterrent nor a substitute;

in fact it had a "built-in deadlock." A United Nations force would be difficult and Sharett felt that there was a greater need for both self-defence and a mutual defence alliance. Israel had the feeling that its survival was being risked for gains in the Arab world.[16] Pearson and Comay had also discussed the Commons debates and agreed that the Opposition had been supporting the arms embargo issue in spite of their professed pro-Israel stands.[17] Comay later noted that at his meeting with Léger over the Eden-Lloyd talks, concern had been expressed for the Middle East and the importance of oil to Britain, as well as possibilities under the tripartite declaration.[18]

The Opposition was relentless in its criticism. In an exchange with its leader George Drew, Pearson stated: "We, in this Government, intend to maintain the same policy [tripartite declaration] and work it out in cooperation with our friends and under controls at home."[19] Drew supported Dulles, saying: "Israel's security could be better assured by means other than an arms race."[20] The government countered and repeatedly asserted that it was in close contact with the United Kingdom, United States, and France.[21]

The Canadian press did not take a particular line on the arms sale in general and on the Sabres issue in particular. Some newspapers did, however, express a consistent line from the time of the Harvards debate until the outbreak of the Sinai-Suez conflagration at the end of October. The *Globe and Mail* commented on 23 January: "Pending the framing of such [i.e., NATO] policy, Canada's decision to stop sending arms is pointless" in the light of the temporary suspension. Ten days later, the *Ottawa Journal* stated: "Canada's shipments are in fact not enough to disturb the 'balance,'" while the *Montreal Star* noted on 6 February, "Our arms policy should be open." As for consistency, the *Winnipeg Free Press* supported the government throughout and was critical of the Progressive Conservative Opposition.

The Opposition's hectoring continued, and from 6 to 9 March the Progressive Conservative's John Diefenbaker, Donald Fleming, George Nowlan, and George Pearkes goaded the Liberal front bench and were joined by the CCF leader in demanding the reimposition of the arms shipment prohibition.[22] The prime minister had earlier stated that "the situation in the Middle East is such that everything that might affect it is being considered at Cabinet level."[23] While External Affairs officials were recommending partial approval of arms exports to Israel, St Laurent told the House of Commons that the government would not interfere with the Harvard orders for Egypt which had cleared customs on 20 February.[24] Yet Drew felt that the Egyptians were receiving favoured treatment, and Diefenbaker insisted that the government apply different principles to the Egyptian and Israeli air forces.[25] That was to no avail although the government had informed the Commons that additional military equipment and ammunition had been approved for Israel.[26]

At a television press conference on 21 March Pearson defended the arms shipment, claiming "that Israel would be cut off from the means of defending herself while the Arab states would have free access to all the arms industries of the Communist states."[27] An isolated Israel, he opined, might intensify and provoke a preventive action. He further noted that it would not be conducive to peace and security "to have all arms going to one side."[28] Demurring from allusions to Western colonialism, he continued: "I am satisfied myself that, if there never had been a State of Israel, there would still be ferment and unrest in the Middle East because of the surge of Arab nationalism."[29]

Israel's increasing anxiety led to a renewed push to procure fighter aircraft. According to Israeli estimates, Egypt would have a fleet of fifty to sixty Ilyushin bombers and some 200 MIG jet fighters. Abba Eban, Israel's Washington ambassador, discussed the Sabres with Canadian Ambassador Arnold Heeney. Heeney felt that the Americans would give a "Green Light" to other countries while they themselves refrained from supplying the planes so as not to impair their ability to restrain the Arabs.[30] He saw no reason for Washington to object to Ottawa's sale of a Sabre squadron to Israel. In a further communication to Heeney, Eban noted that some American action would help other friendly governments "which are considering requests from us."[31] Following a meeting with Livingston Merchant, the United States ambassador in Ottawa, it was stated that Dulles would not interfere with Canadian decisions: however, it appeared that the "Green Light seems to have paled to a pretty Watery Aquamarine."[32]

Comay and Pearson met on 3 April and discussed the St Laurent-Pearson-Eisenhower-Dulles conclave at White Sulphur Springs, West Virginia. It was felt that the United Kingdom, France, and Canada could supply Israel's arms. Pearson said that the Americans would be willing to release "protective stuff," and Dulles "strongly encouraged" Pearson to supply the jets: both had spoken of twelve Sabres and twelve French Mystères. Still there was the problem of maintenance were less than a squadron supplied.[33] It was at that meeting that Comay made the formal request for two dozen Sabres to be supplied by one manufacturer.

The Israeli ambassador stressed that the odds were more heavily weighted against Israel than against the British in the 1940 Battle of Britain. Pearson understood that Israel's survival was involved, although the request to supply would have to rule out using the jets for offensive purposes. Comay also transmitted Sharett's most urgent appeal and noted: "I urged, however, that Canada should act on our request for F-86s independently of whatever items on our Washington list the Americans might or might not approve."[34]

Pearson asked Heeney to inform the State Department, the Foreign Office in London, and the Quai d'Orsay in Paris of the meeting and to report on any news received. Hoping that cabinet would consider the formal request within a week to ten days, Pearson asked Comay to leave matters in his hands.[35] He also told Comay that there was no need for Premier David Ben Gurion to approach St Laurent nor any need to talk to Trade and Commerce Minister C.D. Howe or Defence Minister Ralph Campney. Nevertheless, he thought that talks with Drew, Diefenbaker, Coldwell, and Stewart could augment their sympathy and concomitantly prevent a lambasting of the government. Pearson also felt that Jewish and Zionist pressure would be embarrassing rather than helpful. Comay subsequently spoke with A.E. Ritchie regarding the avoidance of leaks, and as a matter of general policy the government did not comment on arms matters.[36]

In Israel, Sharett met with George Kidd to further emphasize the need for combat aircraft. Even if Israel acquired seventy-two planes, there would still be an obvious imbalance compared to Egypt's 250. Promising to convey the Foreign Minister's message to Ottawa, Kidd observed that Canada had its NATO obligation and the government was faced with opposition in the Commons.[37] Yet a month later Kidd expressed justification for Israel's position.[38] Meanwhile, at its meeting on 5 April cabinet noted the External Affairs minister's report "and agreed that no decision be taken on it at present."[39]

Norman Robertson, Canada's High Commissioner in London, reported that there was support for Israel's request,[40] and the Paris embassy revealed that the French would be delivering twelve Mystères at the rate of one a month starting in May.[41] Léger met with Tyler Thompson of the United States embassy and made the following points: (a) Canada, like the United States, has not been a supplier in recent years; (b) Canada's position was complicated because the head of United Nations Truce Supervision Organization, Major-General E.L.M. Burns, was a Canadian, and if the Arabs no longer wished to recognize him they could use the argument if Canada supplied the F-86s; (c) he doubted that cabinet would be rushed into a decision.[42] Pearson then asked Robertson to check with the British that in their talks with the Soviets they might ascertain whether they would hold off a similar consignment to Egypt. Should that transpire, Canada might do the same regarding the Sabres for Israel.[43]

While the speculated Sabres sale elicited further questions in the House of Commons, Pearson met with the Standing Committee on

External Affairs on 17 and 20 April. Reviewing the general situation, he recalled that the Soviet intervention in the Middle East had aggravated the situation, which to him was the most fundamental point and, "there has been no indication, as far as I know, that the Arab states are willing to negotiate at all on the basis of admitting the existence of any State of Israel – and surely that is basic to the whole question."[44] The growing imbalance was exacerbated by one side refusing to accept a settlement. On Israel's Sabres request, Pearson told the committee that the United States had clearly indicated that it would have no objection if Canada accepted the order. He added: "It seems to me that some consideration should be given to that party to the dispute which is willing to discuss and negotiate a peace settlement. It should be given some kind of protection if it is willing to do that and the other side is not."[45] In the subsequent meeting Diefenbaker asked whether that month's brokered cease-fire between Egypt and Israel would affect the government's decision on the Sabres. Pearson replied that it would be unrealistic to expect a decision pending a final report of the United Nations Secretary-General's efforts.[46]

In a 24 April meeting Pearson assured Comay that the F-86 issue would be on the cabinet agenda. Secretary-General Hammarskjold's mission to the Middle East, coupled with recent Russian statements, made Comay apprehensive of prejudice against Israel's request. The recent cease-fire had left the imbalance intact and there was the additional danger that the Soviet arms would be absorbed and become operational. That could be disastrous especially if Israel's arms requests were left pending. Pearson agreed but claimed that the public would not understand if the government took a decision while the Secretary-General was in the region "restoring peace." He believed that the "need" fell short of an emergency situation. As part of the concept of competitive co-existence, mild Soviet statements – such as the recent one of 17 April – might be misinterpreted, although they were nothing more than a tactical manoeuvre to gain status as a Middle Eastern power. If the Soviets wanted to disengage themselves from the military side of Arab nationalism, they might insert a bargaining lever for a general embargo which of course would be disadvantageous to Israel. Hence, Comay expressed the urgent need to supply Israel's requirements immediately, to offset the imbalance.[47]

Pearson believed that if the Russians were brought into the Middle East via the United Nations, their falseness would be exposed. Yet as Comay pointed out, Israel's frustrating and unhappy predicaments were hampered by both the lapse of many months since the Czech-Egyptian arms deal and the difficulty of convincing Western states that arms were essential to their own and Israeli interests. While Canada could supply the jets along with France, Washington needed to be more forthcoming in its support. Letting Israel despair would only play into the hands of extremists who along with the Israeli Opposition had shown restraint.[48] A week later in communication with Arthur Lourie of Israel's Foreign Office, Comay noted: "Regarding the F-86s you will have gathered from the report of my last talk with Mr Pearson, that the Hammerskjold cease-fire makes the job easier and not harder."[49] Certainly a less pressurized setting was regarded as more benign for the Israeli request.

In an earlier report to MABAR, the Commonwealth division of the Israeli Foreign Ministry, Comay wrote that "there has been a conspicuous and encouraging absence of any strong opposition to" the Sabres request. He also reported that Drew and Diefenbaker were now agreeable, especially since the United Kingdom and the United States approved, as were Coldwell and the CCF, although some in that party disliked the notion of supplying arms. The Opposition was refraining from taking an adverse stand.[50]

Although Comay felt that the press had been apathetic, a brief sampling does not give the impression of indifference. The *Globe and Mail* on 17 April maintained that the North Atlantic Treaty Organization should still work out a policy. It also asked why Israel or even Egypt for that matter, should not be allowed to purchase jets from Canada. As for the government, it was now "on the spot – damned if it does and damned if it does not." *La Presse* of Montreal expressed a similar viewpoint on the same day. Yet the *Prince Albert Daily Herald* of 12 April wrote that regarding munitions supply, for Canada, "Neutrality must be strict or it is nothing."

Some dailies expressed a "hands-off" policy. The *Edmonton Journal* of 17 April continued to call for an arms embargo, and the *Halifax Chronicle-Herald*'s commentator, Eric Dennis, was against arms supply at that time. The *Montreal Star* of the 18th, however, felt the decision rested with the government. The *Province* (Vancouver) commented on the 3rd that the sending of arms was not Canada's job, but the *Telegram* (Toronto) and the *Kitchener-Waterloo Record* said on the 17th that the West should help Israel to be capable of defending itself. Yet the *Sudbury Star* of the 16th feared that arms supply might lead to an arms race. Still the Israeli ambassador claimed that there was surprisingly little editorial comment.[51]

United Nations Truce Supervision Organization head, General Burns, was one recalcitrant Canadian on the issue of the Sabres sale. As an international public servant and former federal deputy minister, Burns was highly regarded by government and Opposition alike, although Israelis did not consider him particularly sympathetic to them.

Arthur Lourie met with him in Israel on 30 April to ascertain his attitude. On the other side, Ambassador Kirkwood in Cairo reported that Burns felt that the Israelis in their truculence might be encouraged to settle the issue by force.[52] In a subsequent report to External Affairs, Kirkwood noted Egypt's obvious opposition to the sale and to the concept of "balanced forces." He claimed that Egypt had no aggressive intentions.[53]

The question of Canadians being recruited for military service in Israel again cropped up in the spring of 1956. An exchange of memoranda in the Consular, Commonwealth and Middle East, Legal, and Defence Liaison divisions stated that "there was nothing in the Citizenship Act which prevents a Canadian citizen from enlisting or serving in the Israeli forces."[54] In "the present emergency," no steps had been taken on limiting the issuance of passports to anyone wishing to enlist in Israeli or Arab forces.[55]

The Canadian government tried to discourage Canadians from serving in Israel's war of independence although Prime Minister King said on 3 April 1948 that no action would be taken "to restrain Canadians from participating in the war."[56] Nevertheless, he approved a proposal to refer passport applicants intending to go to Palestine to the Security Council Resolution of 17 April 1948 calling on governments to refrain from "assisting and encouraging the entry of fighting personnel." Applications of military age men intending to go to Palestine were in fact held up until after the 20 July 1949 signing of the various armistice agreements. That, however, was not a major impediment since intending applicants merely gave other countries as their destination. The provisions of the 1937 Foreign Enlistments Act were not a barrier.

In a lengthy memorandum prepared by the legal division of External Affairs concerning the Foreign Enlistment Act of 1937 (Revised 1952), J.S. Nutt claimed that in this instance the provisions were operative. He stated, however, that it was a "tentative opinion" and "we should refrain from making statements on the effect of the Foreign Enlistments Act, 1937, pending agreement on a common interpretation of the Act."[57] Were a determination necessary it would be left to an Order in Council.[58]

Pearson on 10 May reported to the prime minister on his discussions with Dulles in Paris. The United States had decided that it would shortly release miscellaneous military supplies but no aircraft. The imbalance and the danger from extremists on both sides were clearly growing. The balance-conscious United States felt that some supplies had to go to Egypt as well. The Americans, however, also believed that a number of jet interceptors had to reach Israel – but not from the United States – primarily because of "their anxiety not to be identified conclusively with the Israeli side and not to participate in an arms race, which would not be so much between Israel and Egypt as between the Soviet Union and the United States."[59]

During May Dulles had informed Pearson that the United States intended to have two or three Sabre squadrons available at nearby American controlled bases which could reach Israel within an hour or two should it become a victim of aggression. This, however, would hardly be useful if fifty or sixty planes landed near Tel Aviv with no Israeli pilots trained to fly them. Such basic training could be provided if Canada would now supply the aircraft. According to Pearson Canada was also anxious not to be identified with one side or the other but wanted to assist in preserving the peace. That required the tripartite powers to act quickly and effectively through the United Nations, even bringing the Soviet Union into consultation, an idea he repeated to the NATO council. The United Kingdom was also trying to convince the dual Soviet leadership of Nikolai Bulganin and Nikita Krushchev that they were playing with fire in the Middle East. Still Dulles emphasized that if Canada found it possible to send at least half the Israeli order, it would be important and constructive given the MIGS going to the other side. He did not think the Arabs could complain seriously. As Pearson concluded, the Dulles view would have a bearing on the decision "we will have to make shortly."[60]

On 14 May Léger sent Pearson a memorandum on the "Political Factors Governing A Decision To Export Jet Interceptor Aircraft To Israel." In favour, he stated that (1) Israel was justified in defending itself; (2) the Israeli fear psychology; (3) the Americans were anxious to see others sell the aircraft; (4) Nasser might be engaged in blackmail; (5) the F-86s were defensive aircraft. The negative factors were: (1) Canada's relations with the Arabs would suffer; (2) Burns had been an example of the best role for Canada and opposed the sale of these craft; (3) United Nations officials were opposed, claiming that Israel had caused the recent troubles; (4) Afro-Asians looked upon Israel as an imperialist stronghold; (5) if Israel were supplied it should be by the United Kingdom, France, and Canada as well as the United States; otherwise, Canada might look like another willing satellite such as Czechoslovakia which had sent arms instead of the Soviet Union; (6) contribution by several Western powers would help so Canada would not look as if it were leading the pack; (7) Soviet Union involvement with arms control; (8) the sale of F-87s [sic] could arouse public controversy in Canada. During the debate on the Harvards, the government gave the impression of not wanting to export substantial quantities of arms to the Middle East.[61]

Pressure continued to build over Israel's apprehension that the

Egyptians had already acquired some 250 Soviet jet bombers and fighters. There was the additional concern that the Sabres sale issue would be affected by the seething pipeline debate in the Commons as its ramifications were gripping the Canadian body politic. Comay continued to express Israel's worry to Pearson at their Victoria Day meeting on 21 May, particularly in the wake of the North Atlantic Treaty Organization Paris gathering. Comay subsequently wrote that there was a need to "stall" for several more weeks because the F-86 sale would make sensational world-wide headlines, further provoking the Egyptians to acquire additional arms. Dulles' position in Paris certainly did not make it easy for Canada, because if the United States had "participated officially" in a collective action to directly supply Israel, then Canada would have had less difficulty approving the sale.[62] That seemed to be confirmed by A.E. Ritchie, who attended the meeting wherein Pearson "emphasized that domestic political considerations in Canada were not responsible for delaying the Government's decision ... [and the delay] implied no weakening of support in Canada for the existence of the state of Israel."[63]

Pearson's allusion to non-domestic factors seemed to substantiate the Dulles and allied factors in the Sabres equation. Norman Robertson informed Pearson of having told Selwyn Lloyd that the Canadian government had been encouraged by the United States but was not helpful. The impression, including that within the American press, was that the United States had put Canada up to it, and Canadian sensitivity was stressed in the minister's communication to the ambassador in Washington. Pearson was annoyed that the United States was embarrassing Canada through its encouragement,[64] not to mention that the Sabres were of American design. It seemed that the Canadians were appearing as Western Czechs – the arms suppliers,[65] or as Comay noted, an American agent.[66]

The External Affairs minister had also informed Comay during their Victoria Day meeting that the prime minister was very worried but was impressed by Premier Ben Gurion's statesmanlike behaviour. Yet the Israeli ambassador expressed his government's disappointment at the lack of a positive response after the NATO Paris meeting and the delay philosophy. For his part, Pearson tried to assure Comay that Canada was a firm friend and would stand by Israel and come to its aid if it were attacked. Still Comay stressed that there was no fear of an arms race simply because Egypt now had as much as it could use. The Russians were always aspiring to gain a foothold in the Middle East and were exploiting the situation to get at the Baghdad Pact.[67]

Moved by the situation, Pearson wrote to the ambassador in Cairo the following day, "We would find it increasingly difficult to refuse an

Israel request for defensive equipment if it were clear that the Egyptians were determined to continue building up their strength in offensive weapons against which Israel had little or no protection. You should endeavour to convey to the Egyptians the impression that their intentions are naturally important, possibly a major factor in our considerations of these requests without, of course, suggesting that we shall not sell anything to the Israelis unless they increase their imports."[68]

In an attempt to expedite matters, a prime minister to prime minister approach was initiated by Ben Gurion's letter and memorandum to St Laurent on 31 May. Ben Gurion noted that the Sabres request had been on the Canadian cabinet's agenda for some time, while Egypt had received 250 jets, and even Syria had been a recipient. Stressing the urgency of the situation, Israel still remained threatened, notwithstanding its recent purchase of twenty-four Mystères. If, however, Canada sold the two dozen Sabres, then France might come forward with an additional twenty-four: otherwise, France could feel that it was the sole provider of Israel's defensive arms. Hence Canada's word was important. Aware of the Canadian prime minister's concerns, the *aide-mémoire* noted (1) that the best that could be hoped for in the Security Council was a consolidated cease-fire and (2) Arab war preparations: (a) Egypt had received twenty additional Soviet jet bombers; (b) Egypt was developing night bombing capacity against which Israel would be helpless without the F-86 jets; (c) Soviet delivery had been speeded up; (d) Egyptian training had been intensified; (e) advanced supply bases had been established in Gaza and Sinai; (f) China might aid Egypt; (g) Syrian-Czech arms deal provided for twenty-five MIGS; (h) Egypt supported anti-Western and anti-Israel elements in the Jordanian government; (i) there was Fedayeen activity across Jordanian border; (j) since the Secretary-General's cease-fire, there was still vicious anti-Israel material in the Arab media; (3) it would take several months for the F-86s – if approved – to get to Israel, while eight months had elapsed since the arrival of Soviet jets in Egypt.[69]

In delivering Ben Gurion's letter to St Laurent, Comay remarked that the Canadian prime minister's concern and unease over the pipeline debate was the ostensible reason he did not see Comay and Pearson accepted the letter on his behalf. Pearson, however, was not quite in agreement with the *aide-mémoire's* assumption of the Security Council's limited role.[70] Comay indicated that in the event of the sale's approval, the Israeli government would defer to the Canadian government's wishes concerning time and manner of disclosing the transaction.[71] Nevertheless, Pearson did indicate to St Laurent that he felt that the Security Council was not initiating any move toward a political solution.[72]

As for some Canadian newspapers, Montreal's *La Presse* on 23 May took the line that would have pleased C.D. Howe: Canada should be proud that countries were interested in its industrial products, and aircraft sales were a blessing. On the other hand, the *Province* on 22 May claimed that Canada could readily supply the Sabres from those now in service in Europe, but saw no reason to do so in areas where it had no commitments or direct obligations. Canada's role as an honest broker "is of too great usefulness to the world, including the Big Powers and Israel itself, to be worth losing for our Sabre jets."

Sensitivity over Canada's quandary manifested itself in a handwritten note by the prime minister regarding Czech Premier Siroky, who had apparently erred at a recent press conference when he confirmed the Canadian jets sale along with the French sale. That required a firm denial and St Laurent instructed the chargé d'affaires in Prague to diplomatically point out the error to the Czechs. In addition, Ambassador Kirkwood informed the minister that current Egyptian nationalistic fervour was coupled with forthcoming celebrations, so a lull over the F-86 issue would be appreciated.[73]

In view of the Dulles-Pearson meeting in Washington, Ambassador Heeney notified Léger that given the complicated situation and the need to be ready, Dulles wanted to know whether in the interim Israeli pilots and technicians could be allowed to train at Canadair, the Sabres manufacturer.[74] Léger responded that he saw no practical difficulty in carrying out Dulles' request for training Israeli pilots in Canada; however, it could be politically embarrassing. If the planes were released, then it would be all right to train them. Otherwise, one would be putting the cart before the horse and he was negatively inclined.[75]

No less annoying was a report published in *Falastin*, a Jerusalem Arab language daily, from the Beirut Canadian legation claiming "that a number of Israeli pilots are being trained in Canada to handle Canadian jet planes." That was apparently leaked in Washington based upon Dulles' suggestion that Canada might train the pilots in his communication to Pearson on 11 June.[76] That erroneous report was to be drawn to the State Department's attention "in an informed way ... that such reports are unfortunate and could be embarrassing."[77] A subsequent message was conveyed to the Canadian legation in Beirut to inform the Lebanon authorities that the report was "not true."[78]

With the impending authorization of the Sabre sale, the government preferred non-involvement on the training of Israeli pilots. Hence Ambassador Comay and Canadair made arrangements to train the pilots at Canadair facilities.[79]

A somewhat perplexed and vexed non-resident Ambassador Mac-Dermott informed Ottawa of his meeting with Sharett, saying that the recent critical urgency seemed to have abated. Nonetheless, it appeared that the United Kingdom ambassador was informed that Canada had decided against Israel's request for jets. MacDermott wanted to know if that was so. He added in writing: "First the Czechs! Now the British! *No* one asks the Canadians."[80]

On 12 June Senator David Croll and MP Leon Crestohl went to see the prime minister in the hope that the two Jewish-Liberal parliamentarians could effect some positive movement on the Sabres sale. St Laurent grumbled that others wanted Canada to take the lead, but Crestohl pointed out that France was selling Mystères while the United Kingdom, Italy, and France were also providing other equipment. They knew that the prime minister was concerned about the current volatile pipeline debate in the Commons but believed that a determined effort by Pearson could overcome St Laurent's reservations.[81] Two days later, Michael Garber, United Zionist Council president and Samuel Bronfman, Canadian Jewish Congress president, called on St Laurent with a formal submission. The submission, which requested support for Israel's order, had one element to which Comay objected: that the matter be dealt with at the upcoming London Commonwealth conference.[82] Yet his response expressed St Laurent's sympathy and understanding, and in fact referred to the Commonwealth Conference. One could well understand a reluctance to have the matter discussed at the conference which included members not particularly sympathetic to Israel – especially the Moslems, not to mention the Hindus. The arms request was hardly a topic to be placed before such an open forum with participants of various political proclivities.

London's Israeli Ambassador Eliahu Elath's communication to British Opposition leader Labour's Hugh Gaitskell and British Liberal leader Clement Davies took a more sensible tack. Elath asked them to put in a good word about the Sabres request with St Laurent and Pearson when they met in London. Impressing upon the two leaders that the United Kingdom and United States governments supported the sale would help.[83] In a note on the same day to Director General Walter Eytan, Elath wrote expressing his frustration that everyone brings his goodwill but sends us to another address and the matter cannot suffer delays.[84]

Replying to Ben Gurion, St Laurent stated that the request raised complicated problems for Canada.[85] Yet Comay continued to press Pearson, stressing that nine months had passed since the original Czech-Egyptian arms deal: the "government must embark on a sober re-assessment of Israel's security plight."[86] Léger noted for the prime minister that in light of pressure from the Israelis and Dulles, as well as the issue of training pilots in Canada, the government should opt for a "collective programme" with allies, with Canada, the United Kingdom, United States, and Italy each providing eight Sabres along with the dozen French Mystères.[87] St Laurent told Comay that he realized the seriousness of the matter but that Canada could not take the lead, and action had to be in the context of a collective program. He would discuss the matter with Eden the following week.[88]

The cabinet meeting of 21 June noted Acting External Affairs Minister, National Health and Welfare Minister Paul Martin's notion of a *collective decision under a collective agreement* with the United Kingdom, France, Italy, and the United States, and agreed that St Laurent would discuss it with the British prime minister.[89] In commenting on Crestohl's and Croll's meeting with Pearson the previous week, Comay remarked that there were difficulties with the prime minister and that two (unnamed) cabinet ministers had been opposed but now seemed neutralized. He continued that Dulles' pressure irked the Canadians, giving the impression that they had to carry out the task for the Americans. The Opposition parties seemed all right, although the Progressive Conservatives might be difficult. There had also been discussions concerning used F-86s and training facilities.[90] Concern was somewhat allayed during the Commons debate on supply, when Diefenbaker said that Canada should do its part in assisting Israel, and that an early decision would enable Israel "to maintain a defence, humble as it may be, against superior and threatening forces."[91] A week later he asked Martin about the jets' export permits.[92]

Arab pressure on Canada took a quasi-menacing line as reported by M. Roy of the legation in Beirut. The Syrian chief of staff, General Choukai had summoned one of the Canadian staff and told him that if Canada sold the jets to Israel, "It would seriously prejudice [the] position of [the] Chief of Staff of [the] United Nations Truce Supervision Organization."[93] Pearson's anger was communicated to Robertson in London, asking him to look into the matter, adding, "It seems to me that we have had about enough of these Arab threats of which this is only the most recent and most offensive."[94]

Pearson attended the Commonwealth Prime Ministers' conference convened in London from 27 June to 6 July. British Liberal leader Clement Davies wrote to Ben Gurion that both St Laurent and Pearson had expressed a desire to help but that the Americans were telling Canada what to do while the United States did not send its surplus planes.[95] Prior to St Laurent's return from London, Comay held an urgent meeting with C.D. Howe, pressured by the news that Canadair's directors had said that the company was closing down its production of the Sabres the following month. Comay was also worried that the jets were now obsolescent. Yet sanguine Howe assured him that the F-86 was the best fighter in the world, especially with the Canadian Orenda engine. Pearson claimed that the Sabre still carried the main burden, with which United States Defence Secretary Charles Wilson agreed. While being thankful for the Mystères, Comay said that Israel did not have battle experience with the Sabres. Indicating that Pearson had given the cabinet four reports on the vital nature of sending the jets to Israel, Howe reassured Comay that he should not worry about the F-86s once they received the political green light.[96] In meetings with Diefenbaker and Coldwell the same day, Comay reported that Diefenbaker would at an opportune time support sending the planes. Coldwell was also supportive but there was the problem of pacifists like former MP Angus MacInnis. Nevertheless, Coldwell said he would speak to them and to the party's national executive.[97]

Responding to Diefenbaker, the prime minister said there was nothing at the Commonwealth meeting that "would be an argument for me to put before my colleagues in support of a favourable decision on the request for jet aircraft at this time."[98] Diefenbaker then prodded the prime minister for the reason the Sabres' export permits were being withheld if the allies did not object. St Laurent's reply was that the compelling reasons were the discussions with Burns and the UN Secretary-General.[99] Again the reluctant prime minister was giving significant weight to Burns' judgment concerning Hammerskjold's recent "firefighting" efforts. Coldwell then asked whether the imbalance would not be rectified and was told that "we would have been quite happy to join with other Western powers in doing something to restore a balance, but we do not feel that when other Western powers were not prepared to join in that responsibility left to the government of Canada which has not the immediate interest in the area other powers have."[100] When asked by Progressive Conservative leader George Drew two days later, St Laurent replied that there was a "possibility of doing something that would not be an exclusively Canadian action in the supply of arms to Israel. These discussions are still in progress."[101] Although Burns and Hammerskjold were negative, the prime minister had support in cabinet – particularly Pearson's support – and the opposition. Still he remained cautious until he could move in concert with the allies.

Apprehensive over a possible misinterpretation of the debates in the Commons, Kidd sent a note to Burns about the debate and a message from Pearson which had been dispatched to the information sections of the embassies including London, Paris, Washington, Cairo, Beirut, the United Nations in New York, and Tel Aviv regarding Israel's F-86 application:

1. There may be misinterpretation of that part of the Prime Minister's reply which referred to discussions with General Burns and with the Secretary-General. This was not intended to suggest that there had been discussions between the Canadian Government or the Secretary-General in regard to arms shipments specifically, rather it referred to exchanging views we had in New York on the general Palestine situation and discussions of that situation via the Security Council. When it considered the Secretary General's report and the consequent resolution concerned with the Armistice Agreements in Palestine it was of course important for us to get all the information we could on this matter and *it had a direct bearing on the request for arms which we have received.*

2. If the Israeli Government bring the Prime Minister's statement to your attention this background information should remove any misapprehension they might have.

3. You might also bring this and the immediately preceding message to the attention of General Burns.

(signed) LBP[102]

In a cabinet memorandum of 2 July 1956 Pearson proposed that there be no unilateral release of the Sabres, saying that release depended on a joint or collective decision, and collective action to assist Israel's defensive position by the United States supplying twelve jets and Canada the other twelve. If Dulles was not receptive, then it should be tried with the British, French, or Italians.[103] The following day, cabinet approved the memorandum.

Pearson told Comay about the non-unilateral decision and the desire that Canada not be seen to be taking the initiative in the joint proposal. As for the possibility of Italian Sabres, Comay reminded him that the Canadian F-86 was superior because it had the Orenda engine. But Comay was more disturbed by St Laurent's statement in the Commons that day and asked for clarification. According to Comay, Pearson was also unhappy with the prime minister's reply to Drew. On the "twelve and twelve" proposition, the ambassador said it would be a disappointment to Israel since half a dozen NATO allies had sold Israel military equipment. Pearson countered that the jets, unlike other supplies, were conspicuous and made headlines, while other things could be obtained without publicity. The proposed initiative to the Americans – even if they rejected it – did not close the door to Israel's acquisition of the Canadian Sabres. Nonetheless, the government was still quite irritated by the American attitude even though they had much to gain from releasing the aircraft. Comay was asked not to divulge the Canadian initiative in spite of what the prime minister had said in Parliament.[104]

Editorial comment was supportive of the sale in general, yet there were reticent commentators. The *Globe and Mail* in several comments – the first, on 7 July – stated: "Fill Israel's Arms Orders ... Such a policy would tend to delay, rather than promote armed conflict ... If unrestricted shipments of Canadian arms to Israel succeeded in jolting Washington into adoption of a positive policy, the outlook for peace in the Middle East would be improved." Five days later, the *Globe and Mail* noted the possible influence of General Burns on the government, and the following day asked why Canada looked to the others to provide. The Toronto *Telegram* said on Friday the 13th that "Israel Should Get Jets," while the *Winnipeg Free Press* of the same day wrote that the way to influence Israel was by shipping it arms in an effort to restrain it.

The *Halifax Chronicle-Herald* commented on 18 July on "Canada's Position," again stating that now was not the time to send Israel arms; while the *Ottawa Journal* of the same day, in "Canadian Arms For Israel," recommended that only two things should prevent Canada from shipping the Sabres: absolute North Atlantic Treaty Organization opposition and the contrary advice of Burns and Hammarskjold, "experts who must know pretty accurately the whole Israel-Arab position." In a change from its April position the *Province* of the 19th, in an editorial titled "Communal Aid For Israel," said that aid should only be given in partnership with other Western nations.

The Israeli Foreign Office believed that Burns and Hammarskjold were both negative influences on the Canadian prime minister.[105] St Laurent's replies in the Commons worried Israel and its supporters, and a press release by the United Zionist Council on 13 July voiced disappointment and called for an immediate recommendation to supply. The Israel government's chagrin over St Laurent's statement and Canada's reluctance to supply the aircraft was effectively transmitted to the Associated Press and Reuters.[106]

Since Canada was supplying West Germany with seventy-five Sabres, CCF MP Harold Winch on 20 July asked why this was done for an ex-enemy but not to a friendly country. The prime minister replied that West Germany was a NATO member under mutual aid and that would not have any effect on the decision to sell. In a supplementary question, St Laurent referred to NATO and expressed some frustration, saying, "We do not think it would be appropriate for Canada to take the responsibility of making a decision that it would be proper to do something to which other Western countries do not seem disposed to take the responsibility of agreeing to contribute."[107] Six days later, Diefenbaker asked about the veracity of a press report regarding the finality of a decision. That was denied by St Laurent.[108]

Responding to the "twelve and twelve" proposal, the United States Ambassador in Ottawa, Livingston Merchant, on 25 July informed Pearson that if Canada released twelve Sabres, then the United States would be prepared to export helicopters, machine guns, and scout cars. Meeting with the ambassador two days later, Pearson said that if the United States released that equipment, then Canada would let the twelve Sabres go and the announcement could be made in Canada.[109] That same day Léger informed the Deputy-Minister of National Defence of the possible export of the F-86s: the result of that day's cabinet meeting in which the decision to export in principle had been taken. The decision was, however, deferred until further consultation with the Americans, and then only when the United States shipment had been made public.[110] In a note to the ambassador in Washington, Pearson stated: "I told Merchant that we would not on our part take any action regarding the F-86s without further consideration or until they had decided to accept our earlier proposal."[111]

Against the backdrop of Nasser's nationalization of the Suez Canal on 27 July, Pearson met with Comay, Léger, and Campbell. He said that the decision had been reached after careful consideration. The government did not want Israel to feel abandoned but also did not want to take the lead. Pearson hoped that this would lessen pressure on Israel to take punitive action, although there was concern over some rash action after Nasser's seizure of the Canal Company.[112] According to Comay, the "twelve and twelve" decision might have been a concession to the prime minister and other cabinet elements.

Pearson and St Laurent had adopted the line that Canada would make no move until the United States had announced to the press that in August it would supply helicopters, scout cars, and heavy machine guns. Hence the prime minister could refer to the American releases. Moreover there was an understanding that the French would supply another twelve Mystères after the Sabres had been released. That would entail American stockpiling F-86s at a base near the Middle East, from which they could be flown to Israel in one or two hours. The decision would be kept secret until it had been cleared and announced. Comay expressed his relief and delight, while Pearson claimed while negotiation had been a most difficult assignment, in the long run the delay had been worthwhile.[113]

It had been clear that not forcing the decision before matters had been reconciled was indeed more favourable. Conscious of the fact that a few planes would not be a substantial move for security, Pearson's colleagues had been influenced by Israel's feelings of abandonment and isolation through the one-sided flow of armaments to the area's extremists. Canada hoped that the Sabres would deflect Israel from attempted aggression and provocation. Training facilities for pilots and technicians could be worked out with Canadair.[114]

Pearson also expressed his concern over U.S. rejection of the Aswan Dam Project and Nasser's seizure of the Suez Company. The French chargé d'affaires informed Léger that subsequent to the seizure France might freeze its Egyptian assets, and supply the Israelis with another twenty-four jets as part of the "collective approach."[115] The French, like their Suez Canal Company partners the British, were chafing under the pressure.

In a note to the prime minister, Social Credit leader Solon Low referred to the Sabres: "I just wanted to let you know that whatever decision you reach on the basis of the merits of the situation, my colleagues and I will back you. We will not attempt to make it a political issue."[116] With that it was clear that the government would have the support of all parliamentary parties. Yet Léger in a memorandum to the minister, noted that U.S. ambassador Merchant had said that the United States would not approve the proposal because it did not want to appear that it was in retaliation for the Canal Company seizure.[117] Comay, however, argued that the hold-up should not delay final approval of the planes request.[118] In his conversation with Léger on 31 July Comay noted that both he and Léger had expressed their anxiety over the Suez Canal situation, bearing in mind the Security Council resolution of 1951 on the freedom of passage. Léger felt uncomfortable but doubted that cabinet would reverse its decision. He said that the deal was commercially speaking "peanuts" for Canada, that it gained nothing but created difficulties. Comay doubted any feeling of goodwill, since the cabinet had spent so much time on the issue.[119]

On Saturday 28 July the Commons met for the first time since the Canal expropriation, and again on the 30th. Three days later, after another meeting, Diefenbaker asked whether a decision had been reached on the Sabres export permits in view of the "present truculent attitude being exhibited by Colonel Nasser." Pearson replied that the government's delayed announcement was due to discussions with other governments, and that it had to consider the effect of the recent Suez development. He hoped to make an announcement in a few days. Progressive Conservative George Pearkes asked a supplementary question whether all the Harvards had been delivered to Egypt, to which the minister replied: "My impression is that the order has been completed."[120] That same day, the cabinet deferred further action.[121]

During the External Affairs supply debate, Diefenbaker pointed out that the Soviets have been feeding Nasser's "appetite for aggression" with 150 MIGs and forty-five bombers. He added that "Israel does not ask for assistance in aggressive warfare in the form of bombers and the like; what she is asking for is a few fighters to enable her to raise her defences should Nasser change from mere truculence in words to actual aggression."[122] Alistair Stewart stressed the imbalance in the ability to arm Israel's 1.75 million people against several nations with 40 million: "What we ought to do, in my judgment is to give Israel the aid she is asking in the form of aircraft to combat any attempted aggression." He doubted whether peace would come for a number of years, "and then only by nibbling off one outstanding problem after another."[123] Concerned about the government's procrastination, Donald Fleming wanted to know when, after so many months, the decision on the application was going to be reached, and whether Egypt's seizure of the canal would have any bearings on the application.[124] From the government side came an impassioned plea by Leon Crestohl who several times urged action as quickly as possible in Israel's favour.[125]

In his replies, the External Affairs minister referred to the ongoing discussions but stated that the "view was not to concerting a plan or a collective arrangement governing the shipment of arms to Israel but with a view to seeing whether the responsibilities in this matter can be shared and whether our plans and our policies are in agreement." That seemed to be a partial retreat from the collective action desired in the secret talks and negotiations of the earlier period. Pearson further stated that the delayed decision had been postponed "pending our effort to establish the relationship, if any, of the Suez crisis to the general situation in Palestine."[126] Referring to the previous February's proposed Opposition resolution on an arms shipment embargo to the Middle East, he stated that there would have been no need for such discussions if it had been adopted. Hoping to dispose of the matter in a few days, Pearson claimed the government wanted to be sure that the order for the Sabres would be conducive to security and stability.

While the government considered Israeli requests for half-track vehicles and aircraft parts, Comay met with Howe in his capacity as Minister for Defence Production. Howe gave the ambassador his support and told him to go ahead and hold discussions with Canadair.[127] Comay and other Israeli government purchasing agents met with Canadair officials. Discussions about the twenty-four planes resulted in a price of $325 thousand each with spares at 30 percent of the price. Terms would be between 25 and 30 percent down payment and a payment schedule set by Ottawa. Comay also met with Robert Ford of External Affairs and the Trade and Commerce deputy-minister regarding credit and the export credit insurance for the Sabres.[128]

Attempting to push events forward, Comay continued to prod Pearson on the ominous situation. He met with External Affairs' R.M.

MacDonnell pushing for a decision before the twenty-two nation Suez conference in London between 16 and 22 August in which Canada was not included and which was to deal with Nasser's nationalization of the company.[129]

Léger noted in a memorandum to the minister on 23 August 1956 that Comay had called on the 20th, and agreed that secrecy had to be maintained, despite an almost inevitable leak concerning the United States licences.[130] The following day, Heeney stated that he had met with Robert Murphy of the State Department and had been informed that Dulles approved in principle the licencing of the helicopters, machine guns, and half-tracks. Dulles had apparently been influenced in his decision by Egypt's receipt of three additional shipments, so there was a need for the semblance of counterbalance.[131] Then on the 24th, Comay and Léger met again, noting the United States licences, the British release of certain armaments for Israel, and the French decision to go ahead with the twenty-four Mystères. In the memorandum covering the meeting, Léger added that the United States had still not agreed to go along with the Canadian condition to make the decision public.[132] When Ambassador Merchant called on the minister on the 28th, he confirmed the u.s. release but still hoped that Canada would not link its release to the American one.[133] The Canadian embassy in Cairo also demurred from any Western alliance on the shipments matter.[134]

Prior to a cabinet meeting, France's Ambassador Lacoste informed Pearson that his government had no objection to Canada's supplying the Sabres. The recommendation would delay the announcement and would not mention the French deal. Moreover, Lacoste felt that if Nasser got away with the Suez seizure it would be disastrous for the French in North Africa.[135] That same day, cabinet agreed in principle that "12 F-86s be approved, but that a decision to authorize such shipments be postponed until the time appeared more appropriate": the speculation was two weeks.[136] Comay was unhappy over the delay and told Pearson that Israel's London ambassador had been informed by the British that their whole list – save Centurion tanks, which were in short supply – would be authorized for export.[137]

September became the month of decision and revelation. It was to be a turbulent autumn as a restless Israel began colluding with an increasingly truculent Anglo-French entente. Pearson had urged Selwyn Lloyd "not to resort to force except under the authorization of the United Nations."[138] He communicated with the Paris and Washington embassies that he had explained to Lloyd that Canada was releasing the Sabres in secret. He stated that London, Paris, and Washington "do not want us formally to link any positive decision on our part with any that they have taken or may take and which they hope to keep secret."[139] In a subsequent memorandum, Ford identified four problems: delivery schedule; method of delivery; training; and finally credit, noting that the Export Credit Insurance Corporation would back the deal.[140]

Eban had mentioned to Heeney in Washington that the final decision was "the climax of this Long Odyssey."[141] Comay felt that this was the most propitious time before Suez came up for Security Council consideration; then it might be too late.[142] Furthermore, Pearson had promised Comay that a final decision on release would be reached before the end of September. On the 12th, Pearson contacted Paul Martin, his acting minister, saying that he had considered the matter, and the decision should now be taken if the cabinet agreed. The announcement could be made within the week along the lines that the Canadian government could not justifiably refuse Israel's request in light of Egypt's having received large quantities of jet fighters from the Soviets. The government of Israel had assured Canada that the Sabres would be solely for defence.[143] Martin instructed External Affairs accordingly and met with St Laurent, who was inclined to share Pearson's view on the appropriate timing.[144] Comay had further assured Martin that the Sabres "are for defensive purposes only."[145]

Finally, at 10:00 AM on Friday, the 21st, the following was released to the press:

The Prime Minister announced today that after full and useful discussion with certain friendly Governments, the Canadian Government has now decided that it would not be justified in refusing the request made some time ago by the Government of Israel for permission to purchase interceptor planes from Canadian production for use in the defence of that country. The government has been greatly influenced in this decision by the fact that Israel's neighbour has recently received large numbers of jet fighters from the Soviet Union, and, even more important, a considerable number of modern jet bombers, of which Israel possesses none.

Assurances have been received from the Government of Israel that the interceptors in question will be used solely for defence against aggression.

This approval of Israel's request for 24 F-86's covers a period of six months, during which the planes would normally be made available and shipped. If at any time during this period political circumstances should change in a way which would warrant a cancellation or postponement of the outstanding part of this order, such action will be taken.[146]

At a press conference in the prime minister's office on 18 September, St Laurent stated, "I don't think these 24 planes have increased the tension at all ... if the situation worsened ... the licence can be cancelled."[147]

The government had covered itself with the inevitable "escape clause." The Israeli ambassador issued this press release:

The Government of Israel deeply appreciates the release by the Canadian Government of Sabre jet planes, which are vital for Israel's self-defence. This is a characteristic act of friendship which will hearten the people of Israel. It is at the same time an act of high statesmanship which will have a healthy and stabilizing effect on the tense situation in the Middle East, since it will help to correct the present dangerous imbalance in armament, and deter potential aggressors. Ringed around by hostile and heavily armed neighbours, Israel is compelled to make provision for its security. It will, however, go on seeking by every possible means a negotiated settlement and the peaceful relations which are essential to both Israel and the Arab states and to the whole world.[148]

Could it be that the Sabres would at last be delivered?

The day of the press release, Pearson communicated with the High Commissioner in London, the embassies in Paris and Washington, and NATO and the consul-general in New York, stating: "You should not repeat not refer to Current release to Israel of Heavy equipment, including Jet Aircraft, By any other Western power at the present time. You should GO NO Repeat NO Further than to say that, As indicated In the Press Release, Canada Has Made Its Own Decision After Full Discussion With Friendly Governments Having Responsibility In The Area."[149] Official notification, acknowledgments, and gratitudes were exchanged between Pearson, Ben Gurion, Comay, and Israel's new Foreign Minister Golda Meir.[150] Further benign remarks and platitudes were conveyed when the prime minister addressed the Canadian Jewish Congress meeting in Montreal on 19 October, remarks he would have hardly uttered if the meeting had been held ten days later.

Other diplomatic reactions were readily anticipated. The Lebanese minister called to express his regret. Herbert Norman, Canadian ambassador in Cairo, noted that the Egyptian press was of course negative but not prominent.[151] What raised eyebrows was C.D. Howe's remark in his home constituency of Port Arthur that it was strictly a business deal and he was willing to release aircraft to all countries: to which the *Globe and Mail* on 25 September reacted with "Mr Howe Meet Mr St Laurent." One significant body, the United Church of Canada's Committee on International Affairs, expressed serious misgivings.[152]

Aside from the *Globe and Mail*, which had consistently supported the sale, many dailies gave their approval. The *Gazette* of Saturday the

29th, agreed with the sale, and on 1 October entitled its comment, "Nasser Gets Jets For Israel." The *Winnipeg Free Press* of 24 September, in a comment titled, "Arms to Restrain Aggression," claimed that the sale was a wise and proper move "sanctioning now what it should, on its own reasons, have sanctioned months ago." The *Telegram* of the same date said that the government had acted properly and that the fighter planes as defensive weapons should "serve as a deterrent to Arab ambitions." On the same day, the *Montreal Star* said that the Sabres would "help offset jet fighters Egypt has received from [the] Soviet Union." Two days earlier, the *Citizen* wrote that the decision was "clearly in the interests of peace ... to help restore a military balance."

There were contrasting comments in the major Alberta papers. The *Lethbridge Herald* on 25 September remarked that the "government has done the right thing ... under the $6 Million purchase arrangement through Canadair," but the *Edmonton Journal* of 1 October felt that "the present Israeli government is committed to a policy of massive reprisal ... prudent and human course would be to withdraw approval for the sale of the Sabre jets and reinstate the original embargo." The *Albertan* on 28 September stated that "Israel Is A Problem," regarding the recent raids: "These provocative raids must stop. If not, then Israel must be left to her own resources, to defend herself alone and certainly without arms from Canada." The Kingston *Whig-Standard* of 27 September, under the title, "Israel Erupts," stated: "It is obvious that the Liberal government is deliberately playing with fire in this transaction."

In spite of its decision, the government still had qualms, especially since Israeli reprisal raids made it edgy.[153] Otherwise matters turned to the practical nature of deliverance. Air Vice-Marshal Roy Slemon said that the Royal Canadian Air Force (RCAF) would facilitate the delivery of four aircraft per month, and External Affairs' MacDonnell notified Pearson that the first eight planes were virtually ready and the RCAF would begin ferrying them the next week.[154] At its 11 October meeting, "The Cabinet noted the report of the Minister of National Defence on the possibility of making some F-86 aircraft available to Israel by direct flight rather than by ocean shipment; and agreed that no commitment be made at this time to fly the 24 aircraft to Europe they had planned to send."[155] Yet on the 19th Léger informed the minister that at his meeting with Comay, the ferrying had not seemed practicable, but that any shipping needed to occur before the St Lawrence River closed for the winter.[156] Still, in an earlier memorandum to the minister, Léger had expressed concern and asked whether Israel was embarking on a policy of large-scale military retaliation as a milder variant of preventive war.[157]

Israel's purchasing mission concluded the contract with Canadair and paid for the first eight planes which, although they became the property of the Government of Israel, were still subject to Canadian control.[158] Ben Gurion hoped that credit could be obtained from Canada if Israel's Finance Minister Levi Eshkol was unable to enlist the required amount from Jewish-Canadian leaders. He had been briefed by "Shimon" (Peres), the Israel Defence Ministry's Director-General and "Mosheé (Dayan), Israel's Chief of Staff that eight planes would be sent initially and the cost of training pilots would be approximately $40 thousand (u.s.) each.[159] Reporting to MABAR on 15 October, Comay noted that Eshkol's meeting with the Jewish leaders had not been very successful but that Israel Bonds money would be one of the financial components.[160] Coupled with the Export Credit Insurance Corporation's support, the funds were guaranteed.

Israel's 29 October invasion of the Sinai, followed by the Anglo-French assault on the Suez Canal, ended any prospect that Canadian Sabres would go to the Israelis. While some pundits were surprised and shocked by the military operations and collusions, there were those who were "not entirely unprepared for the Israeli attack."[161] Kidd had kept Ottawa duly informed of Israel's mobilization and military strength.[162] At least it relieved the government of its long endured Sabre burden, and set into motion a *deus ex machina* in the form of a United Nations emergency force. St Laurent's desire for a less than pristine neutrality would somehow survive.[163] The escape clause became fully operative, thus refurbishing Canada's sanitized image for a mediatory role. But no government can be fully cleansed, as Ottawa was to learn shortly, and it was dismayed in the despatching of the Canadian Queen's Own Rifles for service with the United Nations.

On 30 October Moshe Erell of the Ottawa embassy met with C.S. McInnes of External Affairs, who was both cynical and sceptical concerning the former's explanation of the term retaliation as opposed to aggression.[164] The following day cabinet suspended all arms shipments to Israel, although the public statement only referred to the Sabres. In fact the government had advised Canadair of the suspension of the permit by telephone on 29 October, as Howe revealed to the Commons on 7 February 1957 in response to a query from Progressive Conservative leader Diefenbaker. The suspension action had been taken within a few hours after the government found out about the Israeli army's move into Egypt "in significant force."[165] The Department of Citizenship and Immigration's section in Tel Aviv was to suspend all activities. Care was to be taken that RCAF transport in the Middle East avoid the danger of being confused with the Royal Air Force.[166] External Affairs' J.B.C. Watkins met with Comay about the suspension and why it should apply to the Sabres which had been bought and paid for. Comay noted that that did not apply to the Egyptian Harvards which were on their way to Egypt when the embargo had been applied the previous February.[167] On the questions of withdrawals and international forces, Comay had told Watkins that he wanted to convey his "personal views before the arm twisting by the United States and others started."[168] As for the suspension, the government responded that in the case of the Harvards there had been no grounds for action then, while now there was.[169]

Additional meetings with Ford and Watkins were to no avail. A.E. Ritchie felt that the four Israeli pilots training at Canadair with RCAF permission should continue; however, he subsequently learned that they had left for Israel the day before the beginning of the military operation against Egypt.[170] There would be no Canadian F-86s on the Israeli horizon.

The Israelis appeared dismayed that the suspension applied to all twenty-four Sabres, but the Canadian government felt that the Israelis were under an illusion here. Yet, there was nothing illusory about the fact that the Sabres sale was virtually dead so the best thing was to try and retrieve the money for the eight planes. At a meeting with the under-secretary, Comay requested return of the $4 million deposited with Canadair. The request was also made to David Golden, Deputy-Minister of Defence Production.[171] Léger said that he would show the letter to Canadair, although the matter was between Israel and Canadair.[172] A settlement was worked out whereby the Israelis would pay expenses and receive the balance.[173]

When Diefenbaker, who had succeeded Drew as PC leader in December, queried Howe, he replied that although the Canadian government had suspended the order, the cancellation was at the initiative of the government of Israel, and the planes were turned back to the RCAF.[174]

It seems puzzling that Israel's persistence in pursuit of the Sabres was less than full hearted in view of its Mystère acquisition, regarded as equivalent aircraft. Whatever planes it could secure were felt to be legitimate in the light of the Egyptian arsenal. Israel must have been fully aware that Canada's cautious middle-power sensitivities would preclude exportation whether or not anything more than a reprisal raid was justified. What few people knew at the time was that the Anglo-French-Israel collusion was in operation and the French in particular were far more committed than the British to the Israelis.

Ben Gurion in retrospect noted that "by the time we received the Canadian answer, we were already receiving the much needed aircraft from France ... It was not worthwhile using different models ... different spare parts and maintenance methods, and so we turned down the Canadian planes."[175] Had the Israeli ambassador flogged a dead horse? It is hardly logical that twenty-four Sabres would have been refused.

Arthur Lourie, who in 1957 succeeded Comay in Ottawa when he became Israel's representative to the United Nations, asked about Eshkol and the Sabres: why had the Finance minister pushed for funding the F-86s at a time when he knew that Israel was no longer interested in them?[176] But Eshkol knew that although the Israelis would have liked to have the Sabres, any major action on their part would scuttle the negotiations. As for Canadian foreign policy at the time, one savant remarked, "The experience of 1956 renewed the Canadian interest in seeking the security of the Middle East in neutrality."[177] One, however, does not always find what one seeks.

To conclude one could say that while others in Europe and the Middle East engaged in "sabre rattling," particularly over Hungary, the only "sabre rattling" in Canada was possibly a loose part left inside an empty F-86 crate at a Canadair depot.

7 In the Aftermath of Sinai-Suez

"Suez was the unanticipated war; Sinai was not."[1] Thirty years after Sinai-Suez Israel's president Chaim Herzog described it as a watershed in Israel's history.[2] It was also a watershed in Canada's role as a prominent ad hoc innovator or perhaps an international fire-fighter and pacific settler of disputes. It did result in a Nobel Peace Prize for Lester Pearson's part and again highlighted Canada's principal role in the international diplomatic arena.

The conflict "resulted in Israel's military victory and Egypt's political triumph, with the British and French emerging as the politically subdued losers. The United States effectively ended Britain and France's imperial careers in the Middle East, while Israel gained more than a decade of tranquillity and freedom of passage through the Straits of Tiran, a major aim of the operation. As for Nasser, his prize was the undisputed leadership of the Arab world."[3] Moreover, the ambiguity of the Eisenhower-Dulles policy was a vital factor in the pre- and post-conflict eras.

Prudential diplomacy *vis-à-vis* Israel and the Arabs against a background of anxiety over the disruption of the traditional Anglo-American – and occasionally French – entente propelled the St Laurent government onto centre stage in the drama of conflict resolution. At the first emergency special session of the United Nations General Assembly, Pearson proposed that the Secretary-General submit a plan to set up the first international emergency force. The proposal was adopted in the early hours of 4 November with no opposition although there were nineteen abstentions.[4]

In an address to the nation on the international situation, the Canadian prime minister the same day and again on 15 November dealt with the Sinai-Suez crisis and the failed Hungarian revolt against Soviet domination. Although St Laurent regretted Israel's use of force, he said that "we recognize that Israel have [sic] been subjected to grave threats and provocations during the last few years."[5] He also noted that the government had suspended the shipment of the Sabres, indeed of all armaments.

As events continued to unfold and the United Nations force became a reality, Parliament was summoned into special session on 26 November. The purpose as stated in the speech from the throne was that members would be "asked to provide expressly that the provision for Defence expenditures in the Appropriation Act No. 6, 1956, be used for the purpose of Canada's participation in the United Nations Emergency Force of the Middle East in fulfilment of our country's obligations to the United Nations Organization under the Charter ... [and] to authorize the provision of relief for the victims of the recent tragic events in Hungary."[6]

As expected, the Commons divided along party lines, with the most strident criticism coming from the British-oriented Opposition. Nevertheless, the Opposition did support the United Nations police force concept, which Diefenbaker himself had put forth in the Commons some ten months earlier. Acting PC leader Earl Rowe moved an amendment (no confidence) which also regretted the "gratuitous condemnation of the United Kingdom and France ... [who] followed the unrealistic policies of the United States ... [and] have placed Canada in the humiliating position of accepting dictation from President Nasser."[7]

On the matter of so-called dictation was the embarrassing incident that involved the government's choice of the Queen's Own Rifles of Canada as its contribution to the international force. Egypt objected on the grounds that the name and similarity in military dress between British and Canadian forces could confuse the Egyptian public. The Queen's Own Rifles had already gone from Calgary to Halifax to be transported aboard the refitted HMCS *Magnificent* with extensive publicity. Pearson was adamant over Nasser's obduracy which smacked of an Egyptian veto of the force's composition.

The decision on Canada's contribution was finally resolved by the Secretary-General and General Burns, the force's commander. The government accepted the decision to withdraw the Queen's Own Rifles, while the Egyptians agreed to accept Canadian transport and administrative units, which Burns did in fact need. His successful persuasion of Pearson was due no doubt to the esteem in which cabinet held Burns, who had also served as a deputy minister. Although Canada's contribution was assured, the Opposition and segments of the media hardly remained silent over the issue through its caustic comments.[8]

At the Commons special session, CCF leader M.J. Coldwell also expressed understanding for Israel's position and for having "suffered considerable provocation," but regretted the action taken.[9] Similarly Pearson acknowledged the provocation when he reviewed events in a lengthy reply. Three days later, after having completed his response, the Commons approved the government's request and adjourned. In the Senate Arthur Roebuck, a well-known Israel supporter and Liberal stalwart, spoke of Israel's suffering at Egypt's hands.[10]

The CCF also responded to its fellow democratic socialists in the MAPAI (Israel Workers party), which headed Israel's coalition government and sought support for its position. The CCF national executive stated that no blame would be assessed over the Sinai-Suez conflict and regretted the Anglo-French action, but supported the United Nations. It approved: (1) the recognition of Israel and the lifting of the Egyptian blockade of the Suez Canal and the Gulf of Aqaba; (2) that the Suez Canal function along the lines of the Indian proposal to the London Suez conference of the previous August, of Egypt's right to expropriate and operate the canal subject to its being accountable to the United Nations and the users; (3) United Nations launch of a Tennessee Valley Authority-type program for the Nile basin and re-settlement and rehabilitation of the Arab refugees.[11]

The PC leadership convention of 13 and 14 December where John Diefenbaker, the favoured candidate, replaced the ailing George Drew, called for free passage through the Suez Canal, including Israeli ships, and for the resolution of the dispute through peaceful means.[12]

While Israel was in disfavour only with some antisemitic elements within the Social Credit Party, Pearson was concerned to effect an Israeli withdrawal and the deployment of the United Nations force on both sides of the Egyptian-Israeli lines. Israel opposed any restoration of Egyptian military rule in Gaza. It was noted that the withdrawal from Sinai would be based on a steady reduction of forces.[13] Nevertheless, Israel could not envisage the United Nations Emergency Force on its side of the Gaza Strip.[14]

Golda Meir, who succeeded Sharett as Israel's foreign minister, visited Ottawa on 14 December and met with the prime minister. Meir complained about the attitudes of India's Prime Minister Pandit Nehru and its United Nations representative Krishna Menon toward Israel. In a deliberate Canadian effort to avoid the negative and emphasize the positive in negotiations in order to mitigate the conflict,[15] St Laurent took the criticism in his stride and throughout their discussion implied no criticism of Israel's actions.

Parliament dissolved on 14 April. Before the 10 June general election Opposition leader Diefenbaker wanted to know what Canada's attitude and policy would be in the light of the recently announced American policy called the Eisenhower doctrine,[16] which was to serve as a basis for American assistance to any Middle Eastern state requesting assistance in case of attack by a Soviet or Soviet dominated country. Pearson replied on 14 January that the American president's statement contained the following four points: (1) "any assistance against aggression would be given only at the request of the state attacked; (2) any obligation to give such assistance is restricted to overt aggression by any nation controlled by international communism; (3) – and this is of some importance – any measures taken must be consistent with the Charter of the United Nations; and I take it that would mean either positive or negative action by the United Nations. The fourth point is that the measure to be taken or envisaged would be 'subject to the overriding authority of the United Nations Security Council in accordance with the charter.'"[17] The minister noted that the doctrine did not deal with conflicts between non-communist Middle Eastern states, "nor does it deal with communist subversion brought about by non-military means."[18] In particular he stated that the ideas behind the doctrine were welcomed by the government.[19] Two months later, the United States Congress approved the doctrine.

Pearson had hoped that in the wake of the autumn's events, and until a political settlement could be achieved, the United Nations Emergency Force could be a stabilizer "along the Boundary between Egypt and Israel; perhaps also for a time in the Gaza strip."[20] This presaged a quasi-administrative role for the force in the strip that would have involved the need for some sort of security assurance to Israel in obtaining its withdrawal from Gaza and Sharm-el-Sheikh at the Straits of Tiran and in the Gulf of Aqaba.

In the light of Secretary-General Dag Hammarskjold's recent report, pressure continued to build for Israel's withdrawal – pressure coupled with the threat of sanctions to gain its compliance. On 16 January Comay and Eban met with Pearson after he had spoken with U.S. representative Henry Cabot Lodge, Jr, at the United Nations. The two agreed to avoid votes in the General Assembly until the matters of freedom of passage and the stationing of the emergency force in Sharm-el-Sheikh had been dealt with. The following week the Americans and Canadians would press Hammarskjold to desist from action until Pearson's forthcoming speech in which he would bring his ideas into sharper focus at the United Nations. The Americans' agreement with Pearson's notions suited Israel's purpose and in particular its security concerns.[21]

Pearson's General Assembly speech of 18 January noted reports and resolutions regretting Israel's failure to comply with withdrawal requests, and he stated that "we would also regret and be concerned about a withdrawal merely to the old state of affairs ... Surely there must be no return to the conditions, if we can avoid it, which helped to provoke the initial military action."[22] He reminded the Assembly of his speech of 1 and 2 November that a return to the *status quo ante* would be a return not to security but to terror, bloodshed, strife, etc. Stressing as a matter of priority the need to deal with "other matters" than the complete withdrawal of Israel's forces – as noted in the Secretary-General's report – Pearson in his sincerity to change the old cycle of violence called for additional action that could be indicated in subsequent Secretary-General reports. He concluded on an optimistic note anticipating movement to stabilize conditions, enabling greater assurances to encourage Israel to completely withdraw.

Comay reported on 27 January on his discussion with Pearson and his advisors about the United Nations force guarantee of the freedom of passage in the Gulf of Aqaba and through the Straits of Tiran. The ambassador felt that Pearson was a loyal friend and would help Israel on the security matter.[23]

In another statement before the General Assembly, Pearson re-iterated the need to discuss the issues of Israeli withdrawal and arrangements for security and freedom of navigation. He suggested that the emergency force be placed on both the Egyptian and Israeli sides of the demarcation lines and in Gaza, and "that the United Nations should be associated with steps *to replace the present civilian administration of the Gaza strip* and to ensure that that area will not in the future be used as a base or as a target for raids and retaliations."[24] Pearson's proposal was both innovative and designed to get Egypt and Israel to assert that they would not act belligerently or interfere with navigation.

Again on 2 February Pearson presented the Canadian preference to the General Assembly. Hesitatingly, Canada voted for the two resolutions calling for Israeli withdrawal and the creation of peaceful conditions as noted in the Secretary-General's report of 24 January.[25] The External Affairs minister was apprehensive that the implied positive inference in Hammarskjold's report would fall by the wayside, that his more positive aims – particularly the administrative role for the United Nations force in the Gaza strip – might not be realized in spite of his urging to the Assembly.[26] Pearson's apprehensions were not unfounded and were due to the constraints of the political situation and the legalistic approach of the Secretary-General, a legalistic approach which limited the range of any attempt in crisis solving. "In this respect the restoration of sovereignty took precedence over any more positive action; the inevitable result was to support the Egyptian case."[27]

The Commons debate on "the Address" continued with members venting some rather harsh comments; including Progressive Conservative Julian Ferguson's call for Israel to "take another sock at them and clean them up properly."[28] In a pro-Israel speech, Alan MacNaughton of the Liberals felt that the Commonwealth would not abandon Israel and, noting that Gaza pointed at the heart of Israel, contended that it should not be returned to Egypt: "It never was part of Egyptian sovereignty ... forms no part of the Egyptian economy and it is not needed for the security of Egypt."[29] As for the Secretary-General's report, Diefenbaker asked whether Canada did not intend to support Israel's stand "that the withdrawal should not take place until adequate provision has been made to protect Israel from potential acts of aggression."[30] Acting Minister Paul Martin and the prime minister demurred on that and other questions because St Laurent regarded the matter as a delicate situation at the United Nations and wanted to leave it in Pearson's hands.[31]

The situation heated up in Commons as the Committee of Supply considered a loan of $1 million to the United Nations to finance clearance of the Suez Canal. The Leader of the Opposition demanded whether Nasser would allow free passage to all countries including Israel, what guarantees Israel would have, and what Canadian policy was.[32] The CCF's Harold Winch raised similar points. While Finance minister Walter Harris defended the presentation, PC stalwart and future External Affairs minister Howard Green stated that in Parliament there were a few words of "maudlin sympathy for Israel, while at New York the Canadian representative is insisting that Israel must get out of the Gaza strip and away from the Gulf of Aqaba before anything can be done. Could there be any situation more ridiculous?"[33] He chided the government for doing nothing and allowing matters to drift so as to force Israel to withdraw, after which Nasser would demand that the United Nations Emergency Force withdraw,[34] a prescient view of events that came to fruition ten years later.

Under constant peppering by Diefenbaker and Green, the prime minister maintained that the formulation of United Nations resolutions could not yet be divulged as the solution could be disadvantageous and unalterable. Yet the Opposition leader insisted that his party had advanced the idea that before evacuating, "Israel had the right to an assurance that she would not be left unprotected."[35] Moreover, he noted that the Secretary-General interpreted his mandate as not going beyond getting Israel to withdraw. St Laurent, however, expressed his trust in Pearson's "discretion and tact."[36] Still, PC Gordon Churchill commented that the proposed General Assembly resolution (of 2 February) was the pre-eminent "if" factor. He called for priority to be given to the second resolution before insistence on Israel's withdrawal.[37]

Again in the Commons Committee of Supply Diefenbaker tried to elicit some assurance from Finance Minister Walter Harris about the loan, its conditions of repayment, whether all nations including Israel would be allowed free passage once the canal had been cleared, and whether Nasser was prepared to guarantee free passage. Harris could only be hopeful.[38] As for Egypt's demand for the imposition of sanctions on Israel, PC Michael Starr wanted to know what Canada's attitude to the loan would be if the UN voted for economic sanctions.[39] Pearson again hedged, saying, "The attitude the government would have to take – and it would have to give the matter very serious consideration – would depend upon the form in which the question was put to the United Nations. Until we are clear on that point surely I could not be expected to state the opinion or the policy of the government in this matter."[40]

The issue of sanctions continued to have impact on the government and Parliament. That was the concern of an 11 February meeting of Comay, Pearson, and Léger.[41] An unusual separate statement issued outside parliament by CCF leader Coldwell was intended to stress his party's categorical support for Israel. Regarding guarantees against Egyptian border raids and freedom of passage through the Gulf of Aqaba, Coldwell stated that sanctions were "unfair to Israel and shortsighted from the point of world peace ... Israel had ample provocation for her action in marching into Sinai ... Egypt's insistence that Israel be made to obey United Nations resolutions [while it had] hampered Israel's shipping without lawful excuse. Egypt's insistence that Israel be made to obey United Nations resolutions sounds no less than cynical coming as it does from a government which for years ignored and flouted the Security Council and the United Nations when they ordered free passage for Israel's ships through Suez."[42]

Coldwell rejected double standards of morality, one which imposed sanctions on the Jewish state while the other ignored some nations' refusal to respect and comply with UN decisions: "This is not the high intended morality which sought expression in the United Nations Charter, and Canada should say so in no uncertain terms." Time had not run out for a strong United Nations "that will itself strengthen the United Nations Emergency Force and guarantee the integrity of Israel's borders and the borders of all states in the Middle East; time to declare that the United Nations Emergency Force will not withdraw from the

Middle East until there is a permanent peace settlement; time to show that the United Nations is an effective force and will strengthen all its organs for the preservation of peace throughout the world; time to enthrone justice and normality in place of power politics as the force in international affairs." He felt Canada had a unique position in the world to seek effective action.[43] Coldwell had planned to make such a high-minded and forthright statement in the Commons, but time was not available. However, a special statement at times gains greater public attention than any parliamentary comment.

In a follow-up statement, Coldwell asked Pearson to bring the Commons up to date on Israel's position and the likelihood of settlement. While Pearson considered it inappropriate to make a statement in view of the General Assembly's discussions and the need to work out proposals, he did not think that sanctions pressure on Israel to withdraw would be required, and that it would "be both premature and unwise" to propose sanctions without the "necessity of ensuring that the withdrawal should not be to the state of affairs which existed last October."[44] The Social Credit leader received a similar reply from the acting minister two days later.[45]

While tension continued to mount, Pearson appeared before the General Assembly on 26 February and presented Canada's plan to break the deadlock on sanctions and withdrawal. Noting Israeli and Arab fears of elimination and expansion, he reiterated scrupulous observance of the 1949 armistice agreements, arrangements by the Secretary-General and the emergency force's commander for deployment along the armistice demarcation line, no interference with the freedom of innocent passage through the Gulf of Aqaba and the Straits of Tiran, and finally the former mandated territory of Gaza. Dwelling on Gaza and the need for United Nations third party interposition, he recommended that after Israel's withdrawal "the UN should in our view and by agreement with Egypt, accept responsibility to the maximum possible extent for establishing and maintaining effective civil administration in the territory; in fostering economic development and social welfare, in maintaining law and order. UNRWA is already there, with an experienced and efficient administrative nucleus. The United Nations could also provide other help through the United Nations technical assistance machinery, the resources of its Secretariat, and expert consultants recruited for specific purposes. In this way there would be built up in Gaza, in cooperation with Egypt and Israel, a United Nations civil administration."[46] Pearson suggested that the Secretary-General might appoint a United Nations commissioner for Gaza, and felt that "perhaps in this way only, we should be able to effect the withdrawal of Israel." Since the Gaza strip did not belong to any neighbouring state's sovereign territory, he concluded by saying this his program was submitted in the spirit of a "constructive compromise."[47]

While Pearson was presenting his plan to the General Assembly, Diefenbaker questioned the government on its attitude toward the imposition of sanctions if the General Assembly did not accept the Pearson plan. The prime minister's reply was that the dispatch on Pearson's statement that morning to the General Assembly "clearly indicates that we do not think sanctions are justified at this moment."[48] Although Pearson's plan might have been regarded as intrinsically sound, it was ineffectual in the power play of international politics.

Yet the play of power, and particularly American power, took effect. Golda Meir addressed the General Assembly on Friday, 1 March, stating "that Israel would withdraw its forces from Gaza on the assumption that Gaza's administration would remain exclusively in the hands of the United Nations."[49] The prompt and full withdrawal from Sharm-el-Sheikh and the Gaza strip would be in compliance with the General Assembly's first resolution of 2 February.

The central factor in Israel's compliance was the menacing pressure of the Eisenhower-Dulles administration: "Israel's evacuation of Sinai ... followed massive United States pressure, including threats to terminate all United States government aid, and to eventually expel Israel from the U.N."[50] Officially, the basic document was the State Department's aide-mémoire to the Israeli ambassador in Washington in which "best efforts" would be made to have the emergency force move into Gaza. In addition there was a U.S. declaration that its registered vessels would be ready to exercise the right of free and innocent passage in the Gulf of Aqaba and through the Straits of Tiran. While Pearson's 26 February plan if effected might have won Israeli compliance to withdraw, it was the United States government's pressure which did the trick. Arrangements were worked out between General Burns and Israeli Chief of Staff Lt General Moshe Dayan, and the withdrawal was completed within a week's time.

In the Commons, Pearson referred to the Meir statement, that by United States representative to the United Nations Henry Cabot Lodge, Jr., and to Eisenhower's communication to Ben Gurion of 2 March concerning "hopes" which might "prove not to be in vain."[51] But the Israeli assumptions and expectations indeed proved to be in vain. Pearson undoubtedly sensed what would happen as he tried to sound optimistic when he addressed the Assembly on 4 March on the announced Israeli withdrawal – "We have made progress – encouraging progress in the solution of the problem. But much remains to be done."[52] The last part of his comment was to linger for decades.

In discussions with the Ottawa embassy's Moshe Erell, External Affairs' Basil Robinson seemed concerned that Israel would not allow the United Nations force to deploy on its side of the demarcation line. Israel – to the chagrin of the Canadians – felt that there was no necessity for deployment because it claimed that attacks had come from the Egyptian side.[53] That was a feeling many diplomats subsequently held, especially with Nasser's ousting of the force in the prelude to the June 1967 Six Day war. One Canadian foreign policy expert believed the force's removal by Nasser from the Egyptian side could have been retained had it been on the Israeli side.[54] Certainly Israel's military action in the Six Day war would probably have been compromised had it been impeded by the Force's presence, especially after the Egyptian president had ordered its removal.

Egypt's intention to recover its former administrative role in Gaza in opposition to the Pearson United Nations proposed role sparked acute opposition in the Commons. On 11 March Nasser appointed General Omar Latif as the administrative governor of Gaza, and he arrived there on 14 March. Reacting to the Egyptian action, Diefenbaker wanted to know whether the force was subject to the Egyptian leader's "whim and caprice." Responding to Green's supplementary question as to whether the Canadian government considered Egypt the owner of the Gaza strip, the prime minister shied away by saying that Gaza was "a controverted question ... upon which it is not our duty or responsibility to announce what our position is nor would it be, in any opinion, of any help in its solution to have the government of Canada announce what its position is over any kind of lawsuit, especially an international lawsuit."[55] This hardly seemed satisfactory for many.

Social Credit's A.B. Patterson followed with a question regarding the Gaza mayor's statement that American warships were prepared to occupy Gaza to prevent an Israeli attack prior to the Sinai-Suez invasion. The prime minister took that as notice. But Diefenbaker continued to press for the force's withdrawal, and this time St Laurent stated that the government in general recognized "the sovereignty of Egypt over Egyptian territory," implying the need for Egyptian consent. The prime minister followed adopting a prudent course.[56]

Reminiscent of the Queen's Own Rifles affair, Diefenbaker and Green would not let up and questioned Egypt's expression of displeasure with Pearsonian diplomacy in its refusal to allow the landing of Canadian reinforcements for the emergency force. Yet for the prime minister it was a "misunderstanding" regarding the movement from the Naples staging point to Egypt. Again Green asked why the government had not called in the Egyptian ambassador on the matter, to which the prime minister did not respond. Since Egypt had already taken over Gaza, Green persisted in knowing whether the government had made any protest to Egypt. Again the prime minister deferred the matter until Pearson's anticipated statement in the Commons, followed by an agreed day for a foreign affairs debate.[57] In the interim, St Laurent and Defence Minister Ralph Campney noted that once Canadian troops arrived in Naples, they were under United Nations command.[58]

Pearson's statement, delivered in the Commons on 15 March, provided the major defence of the government's policy by reviewing the whole situation chronologically. He regarded the Canadian position as having been consistent since the previous November insofar as the withdrawal of Israeli forces was concerned and since the former conditions of "fear, insecurity and conflict [had] not [been] restored."[59] The minister recalled Canada's preference for a single resolution to the two the General Assembly had adopted on 2 February because the Americans had not "actively" supported a single resolution – a clearly inferred difference between the Dulles and Pearson approaches. Pearson noted that Israel's reluctance to withdraw from Sharm-el-Sheikh and Gaza on "vague and somewhat ambiguous assurances" brought with it Arab calls for sanctions. Canada opposed these "as being unjustified, as impracticable, as unlikely to accomplish the purpose."[60]

Drawing reference to Golda Meir's 1 March statement with assumptions about Aqaba and Tiran, Pearson emphasized the words "take over" regarding the emergency force's civilian and military control of Gaza.[61] He again stressed that a United nations administration would be "not for the administration of Gaza but in the administration of Gaza": to be maintained for a transitory period pending a peace settlement. As for Meir's assertion that this would precipitate a return to deteriorating conditions, Israel would retain its freedom to act. For Pearson, the Canadian position was that Meir's "assumptions and expectations were reasonable."[62] To a degree that was less equivocal than St Laurent's statement during earlier questioning.

Reference was also made to the Eisenhower letter to Ben Gurion and to Pearson's own 26 February General Assembly address. He stated that he did not want to say anything in the Commons that would complicate Hammarskjold's work. Following Diefenbaker's interjection on whether the government recognized Egyptian sovereignty over Gaza, Pearson was more forthright than St Laurent had been four days earlier: "No single power has sovereignty over the Gaza strip."[63] As for the emergency force, the minister said that Egypt's acceptance of the force's resolution (5 November) was voluntary, "by which the Egyptian government imposed on itself a qualification upon the exercise of its sovereignty."[64] Pearson further noted that the General Assembly under the Charter could not create binding legal obligations and could not compel anyone to continue to accept any resolution or to cooperate. Yet it should be borne in mind that voluntary acceptance imposed a qualified sovereignty according to Pearson, and would come up again a decade later before the Six Day War.

Pearson took issue over the Eisenhower doctrine with George Nowlan, who claimed that in case of communist aggression, Americans would intervene. Pearson argued that measures taken by the United States would have to be consonant with American treaty obligations, and "if armed attack occurred, be subject to the overriding authority of the United Nations Security Council in accordance with the Charter."[65] He rejected Opposition charges that Canada had been a "chore boy" or "satellite" of the United States at the United Nations. Pearson pointed out that the Americans had six times voted with but three times against Canada. Canada had refused to sponsor the 2 February resolution on withdrawal arrangements, and "let the United States delegation know quite clearly that we would vote against the Arab resolution of sanctions against Israel, whatever they might do."[66] Pearson concluded by pointing out that the government had done extremely well in the Commonwealth in the eyes of the United Kingdom, France, and Israel, citing the "admiration" Eban had noted in his speech to the General Assembly on 9 March.[67]

Diefenbaker pursued the questions Pearson had left unanswered. If, as Pearson had stated, Egypt had no sovereignty over Gaza, then, "Why should there be on his part an attitude of tacit approval of the entry of Nasser and his legions to take over the civil administration of that area?"[68] Referring to the previous November's Commons special session, Diefenbaker repeated the questions posed on 6 March concerning the use of force over Suez and its clearance and again berated the government on the Gaza strip sovereignty issue. What guarantees could be given regarding Nasser over Gaza, Aqaba, and Suez and Nasser's ending of a United Nations attempt to administer the Gaza strip.[69]

Calling Israel "a bastion of freedom in the Middle East,"[70] Diefenbaker claimed that Israel had to unilaterally accept the promises given it, and that its existence and integrity were subject to Nasser's whim. That could well be disconcerting since Israeli forces had discovered copies of Hitler's *Mein Kampf* in the Sinai, presumably left by Egyptian forces. Diefenbaker concluded by positing a three point stand for Canada: first, the assurance of free and innocent passage in the gulf and canal for all; second, United Nations assumption of responsibility for Gaza to preserve and maintain it from Nasser's actions; and third, reiteration of Nasser's assurance of transit to all nations in the canal.[71]

Alistair Stewart repeated the CCF stand as he had expressed it the previous November: United Nations police action should be extended to cover Israel's borders with Jordan, Lebanon, and Syria; a peace treaty should be ratified as soon as possible; and a solution had to be found to the Suez problem. He also proffered other wide-ranging suggestions including resettlement and rehabilitation of the Palestinian refugees, a Tennessee Valley Authority type program for the Nile to replace the Aswan Dam scheme; and a program to provide fertility in the region by the use of the Jordan waters. He also stated that his party would "not be prepared to submit to the imposition of sanctions on Israel."[72] Known in the Commons as an outspoken Israeli supporter, he stated: "We do not ask that favouritism be shown to Israel. Certainly I am convinced that the Jewish community in this country does not ask for that. All we are asking for is that there should be justice to Israel, neither more nor less ... Israel has got a right to live and has got a right to exist in as much peace and security as is shared by other countries, and we are going to insist that that be a cardinal point of this country's policies."[73] Recalling his visit to Israel, the importance of the gulf, the new city of Eilat and its commercial possibilities as a port, Stewart noted that another blockade would be an act of belligerence. Calling Gaza not territory but an Egyptian colony, he claimed that the inhabitants did not have Egyptian citizenship, and the area was the headquarters of Fedayeen marauders and murderers that Israel wanted to stop.[74] While pressure was being brought to bear on Israel to accede to United Nations requests so pressure should be brought on Egypt, since Egypt had not obeyed the United Nations while Israel by and large had. Nasser should be induced to renounce the state of war against Israel, as should the representatives of other Arab states.[75]

For Social Credit leader Solon Low, it appeared "fantastic" that with its life at stake, Israel would withdraw without definite commitments.[76] Reviewing the past, he reiterated his feeling that the 1947 partition plan had been unwise, and denied perceptions that his party harboured antisemitic sentiments.[77] Nevertheless, he was supportive of the Israeli position.[78]

Health and Welfare Minister and occasional Acting External Affairs Minister Paul Martin defended and praised his colleague. That, however, was not the case with one of the minister's prominent gadflies Howard Green, who in the debate was as critical as ever. He claimed that "the power of moral force has been applied to Israel ... but it certainly does not apply to Egypt."[79] In view of the great danger that Israeli ships would not be allowed through the Suez Canal, Green criticized the government for not taking a stand that the canal must be free to all shipping. Noting the "assumption" on which Israel's withdrawal was based and the non-United Nations administration of Gaza, he stated that in his opinion, "Israel has been betrayed."[80] He urged the government to protest to Egypt and scored it for two fundamental errors: first, the government was too closely following American policy, which was now appeasing the Arabs; and second, it was allowing Nasser to humiliate Canada through the Queen's Own Rifles affair and the embarrassment of Canadian forces waiting to augment the emergency force.[81]

Winding up the lengthy debate, the External Affairs minister responded that the Egyptian press excoriation of the prime minister as an "imperialist" and "warmonger" constituted serious distortions, and twice reminded the official Opposition that "there is no difference between us."[82]

Commenting on the debate, Comay noted that there had been no divergence as contrasted with the debates of the previous November. Notwithstanding the speeches, the Israeli ambassador said that there were two specific aspects of the Israeli point of view which had not been expressed: that the armistice agreements were no longer operative and Egypt had forfeited its right of occupation of Gaza, and that the Israelis were critical of the Secretary-General.[83] While open criticism was unlikely in the debates, no matter how heated, the armistice remained a moot point and detracted from Pearson's substantive proposal to the United Nations. It might also be noted that the day of the debate, External Affairs delayed the export of c-47 aircraft to Israel.[84]

Pearson later admitted that the 15 March debate was difficult and that the Egyptian behaviour had vexed the Canadians. This emerged from a discussion the minister had with Israel's Eban and Michael Kidron at the United Nations the following day. Pearson had apparently notified the emergency force's advisory committee that Canada was not going to be a "scapegoat" in this matter.[85] He also considered it a u.s. responsibility to put every possible pressure on Egypt in view of the very heavy American pressure upon Israel to comply. Under Green's unceasing questioning in the Commons concerning the emergency force's withdrawal to the demarcation line and the admission of Egyptian reassertion of the Gaza strip's administration Pearson stated on 18 March: "The Egyptian general has entered the Gaza strip as an administrator on behalf of the Egyptian government."[86] Moreover he noted that the emergency force had no obligation or responsibility to assist the civil power there or anywhere else. Responding to a report that the Saudis and Egyptians were joining forces to bar Israeli shipping in the Gulf of Aqaba, Pearson was only able to reiterate Canada's stand that Aqaba was an international waterway and that there should be free passage.[87] Pressed further by Green and his Calgary colleague Carl Nickle, the minister said that Israel would protect its own shipping and that the Israeli ship the *Queen of Sheba* had gone through the straits the previous day without interference.[88]

Constant Opposition peppering led on 22 March to an additional statement from the minister, a statement which was essentially a fallback to Hammarskjold's legalistic approach that the Egyptian position derived from the armistice agreements and had been reconfirmed by the General Assembly resolution of 2 February. Hence any function required Egyptian cooperation.[89] Reiterating the government's position that the United Nations "should be associated to the maximum possible extent in the administration of the Gaza strip," Pearson regretted that that was not clear in the United Nations resolution. So the search continued for a "suitable balance" between Egypt and the United Nations. Pearson stressed that the government had said at the United Nations on many occasions that the emergency force had to exercise necessary control to discharge its functions.[90] He also denied a report that Israel was being asked to give up any part of its territory in the Negev.

The emergency force's deployment on both sides of the demarcation line certainly concerned Israel.[91] That matter again arose in the Commons on 27 March, and the minister held to the position that deployment was "meant on both sides."[92] That certainly was a bone of contention between Canada and Israel, and Pearson asked Israel to weigh the matter again when he met with Comay at the beginning of April.[93] Israel might have given greater weight to Canada's request had the situation in the region not reverted to the *status quo ante*. As subsequent history was to show the lack of substantive guarantees for Israel's security led to the emergency force's responding to Nasser's capricious withdrawal in 1967.

In three policy speeches at the end of the twenty-second parliament, Pearson defended the government's policies in the light of realities facing the General Assembly and resulting in "watered down resolutions, or even worse, [resolutions] replaced by 'hopes and assumptions.'"[94] Pearson defended Canada and in particular its actions relative to those of the United Kingdom and the United States. Regarding the u.s., he stated: "On three important Middle East resolution[s] we were, to our regret, unable to vote with the United States delegation on six, happily, we were. We were also not able to accept a United States invitation to sponsor an important resolution, with them and others, because we did not think it went far enough in providing United Nations control in Gaza and on the demarcation line after the withdrawal of Israeli forces. The United States delegation was told that

Canada would have to vote against any resolution of sanctions against Israel in the circumstances that existed, whatever might be."[95]

Three days later, addressing a Jewish audience in Montreal, Pearson again reviewed his government's action and its supportive role saying that "the Government of Israel has also a responsibility. It should, in my view, admit in principle the right of United Nations Expeditionary Force to be deployed on its side of the demarcation line, in accordance with arrangements to be negotiated with it by UNEF. I hope that it will agree to this."[96] Denying any Canadian pressure on Israel to withdraw, he alluded to the vague declarations and reports of the Secretary-General. He also remarked on the Palestinian refugee problem and he felt that Israel should make a contribution.[97]

Diefenbaker and Green persisted in questioning the government's explanations of freedom of navigation in the canal and adequacy of the emergency force to stop infiltrations and incursions. Claiming that the commander of the emergency force was satisfied with the arrangements, Pearson noted that there was still no reply from the Israeli government over the force's operation on its side of the demarcation line.[98]

While Green was tenacious, Pearson responded on the issue of deployment on both side of the line.[99] But Liberal Senator David Croll defended Israel's refusal to allow the emergency force on its territory. In a resolution he introduced on 3 April approving Canadian foreign policy in the Middle East and Hungary and aid to underdeveloped countries, he pointed out that such deployment would be another concession to Nasser, who had made no concession. The marauders do not come from the Israeli side, and the United Nations force would have no function in Israel. As Israel could defend itself against such raids, another concession would only advance the "guerilla borderline" a mile or so beyond the present line.[100]

The length of the emergency force's deployment in Egypt was not clarified during the many Green-Pearson exchanges; according to the minister that matter had to be in accordance with signed agreements. Nevertheless, when the Egyptian president ordered the force out prior to the Six Day War of June 1967, Pearson, who was then prime minister, opposed that unilateral action. The then Secretary-General U Thant succumbed to Nasser's action and the emergency force became history.

Canada continued to delay supplying military equipment to Israel, including the C-47s and the spares for normal maintenance.[101] Pearson felt that the order for spares, supplied by Levy Brothers in Toronto, was too large for release at the moment.[102] In addition to his candid opinion that the Egyptian ambassador in Ottawa was "an amiable fat fellow who is a total loss for any serious purpose," Comay noted

Pearson's description of diplomacy as reliability. The minister also revealed his feelings about Dulles: that the trouble with the American Secretary of State was that he did not want to deceive but that his shifting positions based on legal ingenuity did not foster full confidence in what he said.[103] Pearson said these things just before Comay left his Ottawa posting, and in light of the two men's respect and regard for one another.

Pearson's disappointment and veiled chagrin with the United Nations inability, the Secretary-General's reports and the emergency force's advisory sub-committee, was hinted at in Moshe Erell's meeting with Basil Robinson on 18 April. In addition External Affairs felt that the emergency force would be absolutely passive if military operations were resumed.[104]

Parliament was dissolved and a general election was called for 10 June. Speculation that Liberals would be re-elected would prove inaccurate,[105] as did Elizabeth MacCallum's statement that after the election, Pearson would attack the problem of the Palestinian refugees.[106]

As the senior Israeli diplomat in Ottawa, Moshe Erell attended a meeting of the United Zionist Council held with Pearson on 8 May to discuss (a) a Canadian resident ambassador in Israel; (b) the deteriorating situation in Gaza; (c) that Canada must maintain its stand on both freedom of shipping in the Suez Canal and the Gulf of Aqaba; (d) Pearson's thoughts on the recent North Atlantic Treaty Council meeting and his London meeting with Canadian representatives in the Middle East; (e) that United Nations members could not base their relationships with one another on belligerency.[107] At that meeting the External Affairs minister still expressed the hope that Israel would allow the emergency force on its side, but opposed any reference to the International Court of Justice on the Suez Canal issue.[108]

External Affairs' Margaret Meagher in Tel Aviv reported on her conversation concerning arms with Comay. She noted in her report to the under-secretary "that when they come to us for spare parts and such items, as they have already done, they do not find it convincing to be met with a reference to the United Nations resolutions."[109]

On 10 June the Canadian electorate ended twenty-two years of Liberal rule. Out of a Commons composed of 265 seats, the Progressive Conservatives under Prairie populist Diefenbaker won 112 seats reducing the Liberals to 105 – a loss of 65 from their 1953 election total. The CCF increased its number to 25, and the Social Credit to 19. The next general election eight months later would give Diefenbaker and the PCS the largest majority since Confederation. Unlike his predecessor, Diefenbaker would retain unequivocal control of his government's foreign policy.

In a memorandum prepared for Comay on "the New Government and Middle Eastern Policy," Henry Steinberg of the Jewish Agency noted four significant factors: (1) the prime minister, who had been foreign affairs spokesman for the official Opposition, retained the portfolio and was most friendly and supportive and would not deny his past positions. He was also anti-Nasser; (2) no major changes in policy could be expected but shifts in approach were anticipated; the Tories, for example, did not like the emergency force's arrangements with Nasser and were critical of the Liberals' perceived anti-British stand during the Sinai-Suez crisis; (3) present circumstances and public opinion, might not initiate anything which could be controversial; (4) there would probably be a diminution in Washington's influence and the possibility of a complication if the British shifted to an anti-Israel stance.[110] This had come at a time when the Jewish-Canadian leaders were meeting with the new prime minister. That leadership had built an amiable rapport with the former government and a few were known to be Liberal Party supporters. In the interim, Arthur Lourie was appointed Comay's successor and presented his credentials on 19 September.

The new government made its debut at the United Nations with the prime minister's address to the General Assembly on 23 September, while Diefenbaker was still holding the External Affairs portfolio. With reference to the emergency force, he noted that he had brought up the notion in the Commons in January 1956, and that a permanent force would help to fulfil the hopes of 1945.[111] That matter – with particular tension on the Syrian-Turkish border – was raised by Pearson and Diefenbaker when the new Parliament assembled in October.[112]

Having won a seat in a 4 November by-election the new External Affairs minister and former University of Toronto president Sidney Smith was questioned about the removal of the arms export prohibition on Israel by his Liberal predecessor, and supplemented by Crestohl.[113] The reply signified a plus ça change, plus c'est la même chose. He confirmed the continuation of the previous government's policy "to withhold permission to export to the area any significant military equipment"; meaning no shipments since the early autumn of 1956.[114] As to whether other United Nations members were holding to that principle, the new minister replied that it was no secret that others like the Soviet bloc were exporting, but Canada was sticking to the spirit of the UN resolutions and that included Arab countries in the region.[115]

In some respects, Smith sounded more like a successor to Pearsonian diplomacy than the supposed new Progressive Conservative External Affairs minister. At the outset Diefenbaker had made clear who was the boss at Smith's first meeting with the press.[116] Although considered a prospective leadership candidate in the past, Smith did not have the grassroots background of his leader and his successor, Howard Green.

In his first policy statement, Smith praised the emergency force and the United Nations actions, including resolution of the Syrian-Turkish dispute. He also focused his attention on the "grave plight of the Palestinian refugees."[117] He was happy to report that Canada had been the fourth largest non-Arab contributor to Palestine refugee relief and in the current year had risen to third largest.[118]

In a memorandum submitted to the prime minister and the External Affairs minister on 10 December, S. Bronfman and M. Garber of the Canadian Jewish Congress and United Zionist Council of Canada dealt with NATO and the Middle East and referred to an earlier memorandum of 23 October. The Jewish-Canadian leadership was eager to establish as good a rapport as possible with the new government. The memorandum concluded by recommending: that Canada support the integrity and security of the Middle East as necessary to the collective defence of the North Atlantic treaty; publication of a statement to that effect; security and political as well as economic and technical measures to protect the North Atlantic treaty in the Middle East; and notation of Israel's reliability as a Western democracy.[119] The memorandum was representative of the thinking in other Western Diaspora communities of North Atlantic involvement with Israel as a bulwark against Soviet expansion and influence in the region. This would also have enhanced Israel's security, particularly in light of events since the Soviet intrusion in the prelude to the Sinai-Suez affair. That, however, would have been too far for the NATO powers regardless of the traditional sympathy of the prime minister. After all, Dulles was still in power in Washington.

Parliament dissolved, and in the general election of 31 March 1958, the PCS solidified their hold on power, taking 208 seats and reducing the Liberals to 48 and the CCF to 8. Party stalwarts like Coldwell, Knowles, and Stewart were swept under in the Diefenbaker deluge. The government was firmly entrenched. Ironically, no less entrenched was President Nasser, whose popularity was enhanced when in February he founded the United Arab Republic with Syria.

Yet Middle East instability was elsewhere in evidence. The perennially unstable Lebanon was its usual Syrian prey; Iraq erupted in July with the assassination of the King and with concern for his cousin's regime in Jordan. The anglophone powers intervened; U.S. troops landed in Lebanon on 15 July, and two days later British forces arrived in Jordan. Eisenhower had consulted with Diefenbaker beforehand, and his support led to Canada's approval and participation beginning in May, in the United Nations Observation Group in Lebanon.

In the aftermath of Sinai-Suez and well into the Diefenbaker era, Canada remained on friendly terms as Green succeeded Smith at External Affairs after his untimely death in March 1959. The highlight of that period was certainly the first official visit by Israel Prime Minister Ben Gurion to Ottawa in May 1961.

"Canada did not have a clearly defined Canadian national policy in the Middle East ... The question is whether a country of medium power ought to have prescribed policies."[120] This comment on Canadian policy during the fifties implied the salutary nature of "ad hocism" in order not to be unprepared for crises, enabling the search for a palatable solution not always afforded by prescribed policies. If flexibility was a virtue in the Sinai-Suez conflict and its aftermath, then Pearsonian diplomacy succeeded with the emergency force. Nonetheless, it foundered on the shoals of Gaza in searching for an administrative role for the UN which those in power had no intention of allowing it to perform.

8 Summary and Conclusions

In today's diplomatic world, there is less of a cautious delay between recognition of a nation and its acceptance into the comity of nations through membership in the United Nations, often just a few days between declarations and hoisting of the flag at United Nations headquarters. Israel was not that fortunate, and it took a year before it acquired full UN membership. Moreover, it was more than seven months after Israel's declaration of independence that Canada accorded even *de facto* recognition and a further four and a half months before *de jure* recognition was acknowledged. Some states in the international community still deny such recognition.

The Canadian government's delay exemplified the waning British influence on the Mackenzie King and St Laurent administrations. The heritage of caution was a hallmark of the bureaucracy even with a forward-looking External Affairs minister. At the time, Canada shared with France the political inertia caused by Britain's antagonistic policy as directed by Ernest Bevin in impeding the recognition process. Canada had to act independently in order to retain its credibility at the end of 1948.

The Israelis were anxious to forge ahead with diplomatic relations and pressed on in the period between *de facto* and *de jure* recognitions to receive at least consular status on Canadian soil. In fact it took almost the full decade for Canada and Israel to exchange fully fledged resident ambassadors, and even then, Canada's ambassador to Israel was still not in the country's capital. That in itself is a feature of prudence in diplomacy. Reluctance to move ahead with the relationship was due not only to historical inertia but also to a desire for equilibrium *vis-à-vis* the Arab states still at war with the Jewish nation-state. That led to the second factor of no reciprocity in the exchange of diplomats in the initial period, which Israel accepted as it struggled to augment its diplomatic representation. This reluctance was also a recognition of Canadian Catholic dismay that diplomatic relations existed between Canada and Israel in the absence of formal representation with the Vatican. Third, Tel Aviv and not Jerusalem became the embassy site. Fourth, the delay between a nonresident and resident ambassador was longer than anticipated. The decade from the reestablishment of Jewish sovereignty in the Holy Land until full diplomatic-residential relations was a consequence of that diplomacy.

The forces which converged on the issue of the internationalization of Jerusalem pointed to Canada's adoption of the more pragmatic "functional internationalization" approach. In spite of heavy Catholic pressure on the St Laurent government to support the Vatican position for total international status of the city and its environs, the government held to its approach. The Palestinian Conciliation Commission was powerless, and eventually the Holy Sites fell under separate Israeli and Jordanian jurisdiction. In this instance, Canadian and Israeli policies were not dissimilar, both countries opting for each of the conflicting powers in Jerusalem to exercise its respective municipal functions. Moreover, Canada supported the Israeli contention for direct negotiations to resolve the overall conflict, a position it held to in the subsequent decades.

At the same time, Canada's close consultations with Britain and the United States resulted in no moves to recognize Jerusalem as Israel's capital. The protocol was to resist attempts by Israel to acquire quasi-recognition of Jerusalem as the venue for diplomatic personal contact. Save for the 1979 election pledge of Progressive Conservative Prime Minister Joe Clark to move the embassy to Jerusalem, Canada's position remained intact.

Canada's concern for the Palestinian refugees led to financial support for their care which exceeded that provided by many Arab states. On the overall refugee issue and particularly the claims for compensation, Israel shied away from the issue of Jewish refugees from Arab countries and their claims upon their former lands of domicile. Under the circumstances, the issue did not become a factor in the diplomacy between the two states in that or the next couple of decades.

The armaments question was a salient feature of the Canadian-Israeli equation. The supply of arms by a major middle-class democracy is usually predicated on a reluctance to fuel a conflict in which it has no direct interest and refrains from involvement. Although Canada attempted to abide by the early embargo, it acceded to the 1950 tri-partite declaration allowing limited exports based upon "defensive" needs.

The approach of both Israel and its Canadian supporters was to follow the custom of "quiet diplomacy," avoiding unnecessary publicity. Second, the St Laurent government was reluctant to move on any major items – prior to the formal Sabres request – keeping all purchases minor. Third, there was close co-ordination with the British and Americans and on occasion with the French. Despite sometimes strong pressure from the u.s. and Britain, External Affairs did not always consult or give in, and operated with a display of measured independence. If, however, an Israeli request was bound to cause some friction between the western allies, the Canadians did not grant the request. That was brought into sharper focus in the Sabres saga, whereby France became Israel's jet fighter *deus ex machina*.

In a bureaucracy led by someone who came up through the ranks and was well-schooled in commanding a diplomatic ship through the shoals of conflict, career bureaucrat, highly skilled diplomat, and future prime minister Lester Pearson was the foremost factor in the first decade of Canadian-Israeli relations. From his preliminary role in the establishment of the United Nations Special Committee on Palestine in 1947, until his departure from External Affairs ten years later, his achievements in the ceaseless wars between the sons of Abraham earned him the Nobel Peace Prize. While his religious background had an impact, his pragmatism, conciliatory nature, and sense of timing were the major ingredients in the adoption first of the partition plan and nine years later of the United Nations Emergency Force. He was always highly regarded by his international colleagues, by his Israeli counterparts and their subordinates. Yet his Gaza enclave proposal foundered because he was too far ahead of the more legalistic Dag Hammarskjold.

Pearson was a formidable External Affairs minister who paid close heed to his departmental subordinates in formulating attitudes and policies toward the Middle East in general and Israel in particular. In cabinet he had the undivided support of the prime minister who constantly – albeit not entirely – deferred to him, as to a lesser degree did his cabinet colleagues as far as the Middle East was concerned.

Of the prominent personalities who served as under-secretaries at External Affairs, Norman Robertson was perhaps the most consummate, while Jules Léger was of a similar nature, bearing in mind that the former had been an under-secretary before Pearson. Heeney and R.A. MacKay, on the other hand, were less inclined to be sympathetic to Israel's positions, while Escott Reid was especially unsympathetic, perhaps due to Elizabeth MacCallum's influence. Ignatieff leaned more toward Israel, in contrast to his superior General McNaughton at the United Nations, who tended to side with the Arabs.

External Affairs' leading pro-Arabist was clearly Elizabeth MacCallum. Regarding Pearson as having a "blind spot" when it came to Israel, she nevertheless would not thwart and went along with the minister's decisions. She did, however, at times influence people's negative attitudes toward Israel.

John Holmes, whom many respected then and in his later academic life as Canada's leading foreign policy savant, was a Pearson confidant. He was regarded as objective in his analyses and his memoranda contained fair and just judgments.

As a case study, the Sabres saga is a ten-month microcosm of a decade of prudent diplomacy. Of its five major factors, the first, the cabinet in which the External Affairs minister was pre-eminent, overshadows the others composed of the Opposition, press, bureaucracy and the main antagonists, the Arabs and Israel and its supporters.

At the outset, the government displayed an inordinate degree of ineptitude in handling parliamentary questions. There was an absence of co-ordination between ministers and an inscrutable lack of knowledge about authorized shipments. The External Affairs minister's speech of 24 January 1956 attempted to re-establish some coherence as well as credibility on arms exports to the Middle East by justifying its past and present actions. There was, however, a contradiction in its policy. If cabinet allowed the shipment of training planes to a state receiving massive numbers of war planes, the issue of export for defensive purposes would come into question. The policy was more a question of balancing its exports to the two main antagonists, and hardly defence as was claimed. There was a clear penchant for "non-glamorous-non-headline-seeking" sales of military hardware commensurate with the role of a cautious middle power, and the imbalance created by Egypt's acquisitions from the Soviet bloc necessitated at least a modest Canadian response to Israel's request. Soviet supplies of arms to Egypt would probably have resulted in the cabinet's deferral of the Israeli Sabre request for an indefinite period. Whatever the justification for supplying jets, cabinet was reluctant to act on its own, seeking an act of concert with its allies; it would not have enacted a "go it alone" policy. Nationalization of the Suez Canal Company exacerbated the situation, augmenting pressure to accede to the Israeli request.

It became clear that co-ordination with the Western powers – especially with the United States – was a *sine qua non* in the decision on the Sabres. Canada as a non-permanent Security Council member, refused to initiate any plan and deferred to the tripartite declaration powers. Cabinet would not go beyond a main or secondary role in the supply of arms. Known as interceptor jets, cabinet regarded the Sabres as being for defensive purposes.

Had the other Western powers not increased their arms supplies to Israel, it is doubtful whether Canada would have. The "escape clause" in the decision to supply the squadron was the essential element in forestalling a change in conditions or circumstances.

In spite of irksome behaviour, the United States, particularly its Secretary of State, loomed as the most decisive factor in the cabinet's decision. While maintaining the aforementioned parameters, cabinet was determined to sustain independence of action and not appear as the American "Czechoslovakia." Meanwhile Britain and France were significant factors in influencing cabinet's decision, with Britain taking precedence over France; other NATO partners were inconsequential; whereas the United Nations Secretary-General and the Truce Supervisor commander could be regarded as tertiary factors of influence, the External Affairs minister was the saga's primary actor, influencing while at the same time deferring to his prime minister who was still reluctant to reach a positive decision.

The Opposition displayed shrewdness in catching cabinet off guard and embarrassing it over mishandling Commons questions and answers, but while exploiting the situation, it did not succeed in winning a permanent embargo on arms to the Middle East. As the Sabres affair progressed, the Progressive Conservative "holier than thou" attitude changed and the party, with Diefenbaker the key figure of the parliamentary debate, came to support the sale. The CCF and its key spokesman Alistair Stewart clearly sympathized with Israel. While ideologically aligned with Israel's government and its society, its pacifist wing was uneasy over the supply of arms but backed the Sabres sale. The Social Creditors were the least involved but lent their support to the government.

The press was not a factor of consequence because there was no categorical consensus. The major metropolitan dailies supported the sale; smaller dailies were mixed in their reactions to government policy.

Among the bureaucrats, Under-Secretary Léger was cautious and fairly well balanced in his approach to policy options regarding the Sabres. That could also be said of some of his colleagues in External Affairs. The Canadian diplomats in Cairo and Tel Aviv as well as the other major capitals aided the minister's assessments. Truce supervision head General Burns, an influential former federal deputy minister, was a factor in the prime minister's recalcitrance.

As for the antagonists, Israel's defence predicament held significant sway over the External Affairs minister and was a vital element in procuring the Sabres. Once Israel took the offensive, the sale collapsed. The pro-Israel elements of the United Zionist Council and the Canadian Jewish Congress, including the two Jewish parliamentarians, cannot be regarded as even minor factors in the decision equation. Egypt and the Soviet bloc were vital, and cabinet did not want to alienate them. It is a paradox that Canada shipped Egypt's Harvard order but Israel's Sabres never left dock.

This case study serves as a prism through which to view the diplomacy of prudence. As a major middle power, Canada was an integral part of the Western alliance, respected or at least not unloved by the nations born in the wake of the Second World War as well as by the victims, victors, and vanquished of that horrible cataclysm.

In the formulation of Canadian foreign policy, the cabinet was guided first by consideration for its Western friends, particularly the u.s., Britain, and France, then by the security and defence needs of Israel in quasi-balance with its neighbours, third by the United Nations and its role in the conflict, and fourth by the impact of policy decisions on the body politic in Canada. Finally, Canada tried to stay uninvolved wherever possible, and when involvement became necessary it acted with balance and modesty and in concert with its allies.

In the Arab-Israeli conflict, particularly in the Sinai-Suez hostilities, Canadian policy was one of caution and guarded non-involvement with the combatants. Until the outbreak of open fighting there was a desire to avoid military confrontation and then move toward a pacific settlement of disputes.

Canadian sensitivity to being in a non-satellite partnership and exercising independent decision making was a consequential factor; however, while initiative in arms supply was not a policy precept, maintaining the Western alliance and the Commonwealth certainly were.

In the wake of the outbreak of hostilities in Sinai and Suez, Canadian policy could be classified as "cautious ad hocery." The government's uncomfortable predicament was somewhat alleviated through the establishment of the international emergency force as a face-saver for all the conflicting parties. It rescued the situation from further deterioration and wound up as a feather in Canada's diplomatic hat.

Nevertheless, Pearson's additional attempt to win approval for a United Nations role in Gaza proved futile as he attempted to lead the pack: the trouble was there was no pack to lead. Strict legalism overrode a theoretically sensible yet feckless political plan which could be regarded as an admirable attempt to avoid a return to the hostile *status quo ante*. The true reflection of the pack's intention was the Secretary-General's position. Pearson and External Affairs' disappointment was augmented later when Israel would not agree to the international force's deployment on its side.

Canada's conciliatory approach did not achieve Israel's withdrawal from the Sinai; the United States succeeded with quasi-brutal threats. What became known as the Eisenhower model did the trick; Pearsonian diplomacy had reached its limit.

The parliamentary debates enabled the official Opposition to prod and criticize the government reflecting a pro-British, pro-Israeli stance in the ephemeral Anglo-French-Israeli alliance. The CCF remained solidly pro-Israel but spurned the Anglo-French action. The Social Credit party supported the government and was somewhat understanding of Israel's predicament.

A more aggressive Progressive Conservative leader's popularity undercut the government, whose performance on the international scene was almost in sharp contrast to its domestic role. After twenty-two years of continuous Liberal rule, the Canadian electorate clearly indicated its desire for change at the June 1957 election. Diefenbaker's popularity was overwhelmingly reconfirmed in the following March's general election. That, however, did not herald any significant change in foreign policy except that neither he nor any successive External Affairs ministers exercised Pearson's control. Diefenbaker has been pro-Zionist before Israel's establishment, and there was no change as his government faced no cataclysmic outbreaks directly involving Israel during his tenureship.

Canada had become a major or principal middle power during its ninth decade while Israel struggled through its first one. The process leading up to the adoption of the partition plan, Israel's establishment, and Canadian activities in the Sinai-Suez affair and its aftermath put Canada in a special diplomatic place in relation to Israel. Yet the domestic and external factors which shaped the parameters of Canadian policy toward Israel were drawn with caution and highlighted Canada's full maturity as a practitioner of foreign policy and its respected major middle power status.

Prudence and caution were the warp and weft of Canadian policy in the various instances and case studies. The restoration of Jewish sovereignty, preceded by reluctant support for the United Nations partition plan, moved from a policy of non-commitment to cautious support. It resulted in withholding de facto recognition and delaying de jure acceptance and showed that prudence would not be a soft policy line in this and subsequent decades.

While it was inevitable that de jure recognition would entail some formal diplomatic representation, Canada only granted Israel consul general status initially, declining any reciprocity on its part. Such overt prudence lasted until the arrival in Ottawa four years later of the minister plenipotentiary and his elevation to ambassadorial rank in the following year. It took another four years for Canada to accept a resident ambassador; prudence more than personified.

The various case studies corroborate the prudential theme. Religion was a factor with the Holy See concerning the internationalization of Jerusalem, but the Canadian government did not succumb to pressure on its Roman Catholic prime minister and did not support the General Assembly resolution. In a sense, the government appeared closer to the Israeli position on separate municipal administrations for the divided city, yet it did not recognize Israel's official national capital.

The refugee – particularly the Palestinian – was not a major issue in the Canada-Israel relationship. While the External Affairs minister prodded the Israeli ambassador on the matter, it was done with circumspection. Financial and material aid granted by Canada was not incongruous with the diplomacy of prudence, since it was regarded as humanitarian assistance.

Arms sales can be political mine fields, and even under the best circumstances democratic governments shun publicity on the matter. In the ongoing Arab-Israeli conflict, Canada and Israel followed the basic precept of quiet diplomacy. The 1950 tri-partite declaration was well suited to Canadian policy with its restriction to "defensive" military hardware until the Sabres difficulties. While having been discreetly cautious till then, the government was able to act independently and not always in conjunction with its allies.

Bureaucracies are conservative and inherently prone to follow paths of prudence. The under-secretaries, directors and divisional heads functioned well with the minister, who himself had come up through the ranks. While sympathies were discerned one way or the other *vis-à-vis* Israel, there was never any palpable friction between the minister and his subordinates.

The F-86 jets certainly provided the major case which further substantiated the prudential policy of the St Laurent government. The caution at times reached a level that raised doubts whether the government could and would reach any decision on the sale. The Canadian-built state of the art jet was classified as an interceptor for defence purposes. The Israelis undeniably desired the aircraft, but the dilatory Canadians compelled the Ben Gurion government to find an alternative, which its ephemeral ally France was to supply.

The mere fact that the process stretched out for months says a great deal about the diplomacy of prudence. Early caution resulted in the inclusion of an "escape clause" for the Canadian government. Hence one of the first acts upon the outbreak of hostilities in Sinai was to suspend the sale. The extremity of prudence had been tested with an immediate response as the Canadian body politic began a period of great anxiety. Moreover, the government's subsequent reactions and modus operandi at the United Nations might not have been so successful, particularly with the Third World, had the delivery been made. That period in Canadian diplomacy might be defined as "caution coupled with positive conciliation."

From Sinai-Suez until the federal election of June 1957, the government maintained its prudential approach notwithstanding Pearson's inability to win United Nations approval for his Gaza plan. In spite of the kudos it acquired, the Liberal government's days were numbered. The domestic and not the foreign scene was what mostly concerned the Canadian voters who had decided to elect the Conservatives.

While the Diefenbaker-led Progressive Conservatives wanted to put their imprint on the domestic as well as international scene, they retained the prudential course as far as Israel was concerned. Notwithstanding the prime minister's feelings toward the Jewish state, the diplomacy of prudence was alive and well at the conclusion of the decade and destined to affect the next few decades.

9 Epilogue

Canada's overly cautious noncommitted prudence toward Mandated Palestine and the modern Jewish state's first decade set a pattern for the relationship in succeeding decades. The difference in Pearson's restrained sympathy and Diefenbaker's outspoken partisan support for Israel undoubtedly reflected the former's bureaucratic background in contrast with the latter's Prairie political grassroots. The two men dominated Canada's tenth decade and a quieter relationship with Israel in its second decade.

Canadian response to the Six Day War of June 1967 was indicative of the greater caution of Pearson as prime minister and External Affairs Minister Paul Martin. Prudence in the subsequent Pierre Trudeau and the Joe Clark–Brian Mulroney decades produced a more "evenhanded" policy, for some a codeword for a pro-Arab position. The old perception of a pro-Israel Canada receded more from public view as the Palestine Liberation Organization and its active terrorist branches affected Canadians and others in the Western world. This was aided and abetted by the pro-Arab Soviet bloc and bolstered by the Third World or so-called nonaligned countries.

The Yom Kippur War of October 1973; the Crimes and Habitat congresses of two and three years later; the decades-long Arab boycott, and the Lebanon war of 1982 clearly influenced Israel's third and fourth decades. Of no less significance was the Canadian Senate's report of June 1985, which showed more pro-Arab sentiment under the "evenhanded" policy concept. The shock of External Affairs minister Clark's 10 March 1988 speech to the Canada-Israel Committee in Ottawa was viewed as the most egregious criticism of Israel ever voiced by a Canadian leader.

Despite this trend in policy, the diplomatic commitment to Israel's existence and security, which Pearson began in the first decade and reconfirmed as prime minister during the Six Day War, remained a hallmark of Canadian policy. Subsequent governments upheld the commitment, whatever their inclinations, and stressed the need for peace negotiations and settlement of the Palestinian problem. Canada became a member of the G-7, one of the seven largest industrial nations, and took up the task of chairing the refugee group after direct peace negotiations had begun in 1991–92. It was then that the term refugee would include Jewish as well as Arab within the Middle East context which was not the case in the first decade.

There is a paradox in the history of Canadian foreign policy as far as the Levant is concerned. "Mike" Pearson, the great architect of Canada's external relations, acquired a reputation which is still unsurpassed. While historians and political scientists have noted his contributions to internationalism, regional security, the Western alliance, and saving the anglophone Commonwealth, his prudent support of Israel seems a less prominent part of his heritage. Elizabeth MacCallum's pro-Arab stand was hardly a match for the famous minister's. However, her pro-Arabism outlived him, surviving within External Affairs and in some of its mandarins.

That prudence must be a major feature of any state's foreign policy will always be an axiom in non-messianic times. The degree to which prudence is the hallmark of a state's policy determines its activism on the diplomatic front. In that sense, the first decade of Canada's relations with the modern Jewish state can be viewed as prudent with some conciliatory action, action that became increasingly cautious as time went on.

Notes

CHAPTER ONE

1 United Nations General Assembly resolution 181, 29 November 1947.
2 Regarding Pearson's free hand, see Michael Brecher, *The Foreign Policy System of Israel: Setting, Images, Process* (London: Oxford University Press, 1972), 378 fn. 3. See Michael B. Oren, "Faith and Fairmindedness: Lester B. Pearson and the Suez Crisis." *Diplomacy & Statecraft* 3, no. 1 (1992): 48–73.
3 David B. Dewitt and John Kirton, *Canada as a Principal Power: A Study in Foreign Policy and International Relations* (Toronto: John Wiley & Sons, 1983), 367ff.
4 Israel State Archives, Foreign Office files (hereafter ISA) File 380/11, A. Lourie to ambassador in Washington, 25 April 1958, on the former's discussion with Paul Martin, a member of the Mackenzie King, St Laurent, and Pearson cabinets. See also J.W. Pickersgill and D.F. Forster, *The Mackenzie King Record*, vol. 4 (Toronto: University of Toronto Press, 1961).
5 See Zachariah Kay, *Canada and Palestine: The Politics of Non-Commitment* (Jerusalem: Israel Universities Press, 1978); and David Bercuson, *Canada and the Birth of Israel: A Study in Canadian Foreign Policy* (Toronto: University of Toronto Press, 1985).
6 National Archives of Canada (hereafter NA) File 47/B(S), part 3, 6 March 1948.
7 Ibid., part 4, 18 May 1948; also cited in John A. Munro and Alex I. Inglis, eds., *Mike: The Memoirs of the Right Honourable Lester B. Pear-*

son, vol. 2: *1948–1957* (Toronto: University of Toronto Press and Signet, 1975), 243–4.

8 See George Ignatieff, *The Making of a Peacemonger: The Memoirs of George Ignatieff* (Markham, Ont.: Penguin, 1987), 103 and passim.

9 ISA 2394/41, "Canada's Recognition of Israel."

10 Ibid.

11 Ibid., and NA 5475-CR-I-40, 2 August 1948.

12 *Documents on the Foreign Policy of Israel* (hereafter DFPI) 2, Jerusalem: ISA 1984, *Companion Volume* (hereafter CV) 2:43.

13 The Palestinian Conciliation Commission (PCC) was established by the General Assembly's resolution on 11 December 1948.

14 DFPI CV 2:43.

15 NA 5475-CR-I-40, 1 and 7 December 1948, respectively.

16 Ibid. and ISA 2414/19.

17 DFPI 2:271, Elath to Sharett, 21 December 1948.

18 DFPI CV 2:51.

19 Ibid., 52. See also Pearson to Security Council, Statements and Speeches (hereafter S&S), External Affairs (hereafter EXA) 48/65, 2 December 1948.

20 Munro and Inglis, *Mike*, vol. 2, 245. See also Kay, *Canada and Palestine*, chapter 14; emphasis mine.

21 DFPI 2:371, Eban to Sharett.

22 Kay, *Canada and Palestine*, 140.

23 Ignatieff, *The Making of a Peacemonger*, 103.

24 DFPI 2:364–5, 13 January 1949; and ISA 2598/12, 12 January 1949.

25 ISA 2414/19. See also Eban to Sharett, 9 February 1949 in DFPI 2:422.

26 ISA 2414/19, 24 February 1949. See also Kay, *Canada and Palestine*, passim.

27 Kay, *Canada and Palestine*, passim.

28 DFPI 2:422, 426. See also Eban to Ignatieff of 2 March 1949 in ISA 70/19.

29 DFPI 2:426.

30 Ibid., 468.

31 Ibid., 472.

32 Ibid., 492, Eban to Walter Eytan, director general. The Israeli director general is equivalent to the Canadian deputy minister or under-secretary.

33 Ibid., 551.

34 ISA 70/19, Eban to Ignatieff, 25 February 1949.

35 United Nations mediator Bernadotte had been murdered in Jerusalem the previous September.

36 NA, Privy Council Office (hereafter PCO) File 1-16, Secretary of State for External Affairs to Permanent Delegation at the United Nations, 26 April 1949.

37 Ibid, 27 April 1949.

38 Ibid., 16 and 18 May 1949.

39 ISA 2394/41, 19 August 1949, and NA 5475-CR-1-40.

40 Canada, House of Commons Debates (hereafter HC), 25 March 1952, 764.

41 ISA 2584/19, 30 January 1949.

42 Ibid. 66/15, 20 January 1949.

43 S.J. Zacks, President of the Zionist Organization of Canada (ZOC) and Chairman of the United Zionist Council of Canada (UZC) was irked that the Canadian Labour Zionist Organization had leaked the appointment before it had been cleared with the Canadian government. Zacks to Lourie, ISA 74/13, 1 April 1949.

44 Ibid., 376/13, 24 February 1949.

45 NA 50168-40, 2 February 1949. The precedent was Elath's appointment as Israel's representative in Washington.

46 ISA 2583/1, 11 September 1949.

47 Ibid., 2385/43, 15 June 1950. Harman memorandum on discussion with EXA's T.W.L. MacDermott in ibid., 2 August 1950.

48 John Holmes, *The Shaping of Peace: Canada and the Search for World Order*, vol. 2: *1943–1957* (Toronto: University of Toronto Press, 1972), 127.

49 ISA 2385/43, Comay to Eban, 30 October 1950.

50 Ibid., 22 November 1950.

51 Ibid., 12 December 1950.

52 NA, PCO, 6 February 1951.

53 ISA 2385/43, 1 March 1950.

54 Ibid., 16 April 1951.

55 Ibid., 2584/19, 1 September 1953

56 Ibid., 2419/19, Eytan, 2 October 1953.

57 Ibid. The first Jewish-Canadian ambassador was appointed to the Tel Aviv embassy in 1992.

58 Ibid., 2385/43, 10 September 1953.

59 Ibid., 22 October 1953.

60 NA 50134-40, and 10963-40, part 2, and press release of 26 July 1954.

61 Ibid.

62 ISA 2564/19, letters of 12 and 18 June 1956.

63 Ibid., 3122/25, 6 and 8 May 1957.

CHAPTER TWO

1 S&S 48/61.

2 DFPI 4:556, 18 October 1949.

3 *Canada and the United Nations 1949*, EXA Conference Series, no. 1, appendix 14, 258.

4 ISA 2382/21, Harman to Comay, 13 January 1950.

5 NA 50134-40, 5 December 1949.
6 Ibid.
7 HC, 8 December 1949, 2905.
8 DFPI 4:682–3.
9 NA 50134–40, press conference, 15 December 1949.
10 Ibid., 16 December 1949.
11 Ibid.
12 For example, *L'Action catholique and Le Droit* (Ottawa), 12 December 1949.
13 NA 50134–40, 28 December 1949. The Canadian Congress of Labour had a pro-Zionist tradition and strong support for the Histadrut (the Israel Labour Federation).
14 NA 8903-E-40, Heeney to Minister, 21 December 1949.
15 DFPI 4:773–4, 30 December 1949.
16 NA 50134–40.
17 Ibid., 9 January 1950.
18 Ibid., re press conference of 12 January 1950.
19 Ibid., letter of 23 June 1950. (A similar letter was sent to the United Kingdom, United States, Swedish, New Zealand, Norwegian, Turkish, Icelandic, Uruguayan, Dutch, the Dominican Republic and Chilean governments, DFPI 5:400–1.)
20 Ibid.
21 NA 50134–40, 31 July 1950.
22 Ibid., 9 August 1950.
23 Ibid., Memorandum from Pearson to prime minister, 8 September 1950.
24 Ibid., EXA minister to chairman, Canadian delegation, 20 October 1950. In a message to the chair on 30 September, Léger of EXA noted that information from United Kingdom sources persisted in stating that Israel intended to attack in order to gain control of Jerusalem's Mount Scopus, also in ibid.
25 Ibid, 26 November 1950.
26 Ibid., 14 December 1950.
27 ISA 468/1, 24 April 1951.
28 EXA, *Canada and the United Nations*, 1951–52, 31–4.
29 Ibid., 1952–53, 9–10.
30 NA 5134-B-40, Memorandum for acting minister, 24 September 1953.
31 Ibid., 17 September 1954.
32 Ibid., 24 September 1954.
33 Ibid., 2 November 1954.
34 Ibid., 15 November 1954.
35 Ibid., 30 December 1954.
36 EXA *Monthly Bulletin* 7, no. 1 (1955):18, 14.

37 NA 50134-B-40, 19 November 1954.
38 Ibid., Kidd to minister, 11 January 1955.
39 Ibid., 2 February 1955.
40 Ibid., 17 February 1955.
41 Ibid., Léger to Pearson, 5 August 1955.
42 Ibid., 12 August 1955.
43 Ibid, 2 October 1955.
44 For a full discussion, see George Takach, "Clark and the Jerusalem Embassy Affair: Initiative and Constraint in Canadian Foreign Policy," in David Taras and David Goldberg, eds., *The Domestic Battleground: Canada and the Arab-Israel Conflict* (Kingston, Montreal, London: McGill-Queen's University Press, 1989), 144–66.

CHAPTER THREE

1 NA 47-B-(S)-part 7, 10 November 1948.
2 The "Right of Return" according to one source, Abba Eban, has been erroneously interpreted. He has noted that the matter was one of "permission" and not of "right" with reference to the General Assembly of December 1949. He concluded: "Entry into Israel is something that individuals or groups outside of Israel have a right to request and that Israel has a sovereign right to accept or reject." Abba Eban to the editor of *The Jerusalem Post*, 4 August 1989.
3 NA 50134, 7 December 1950.
4 Ibid., memorandum of 28 September 1951.
5 EXA, *Canada and the United Nations*, 1951–52, 65.
6 HC, 6 May 1955, 3532.
7 Minutes of Proceedings, 25 May 1955, 558.
8 Ibid., 559.
9 ISA 328/1, 7 June 1955.
10 HC, 18 January 1956, 265.
11 Ibid., 468–9, 24 January 1956.
12 Ibid., 31 January 1958, 732.
13 EXA *Monthly Bulletin* 7, no. 12 (1955):316.
14 S&S 57/5.
15 Ibid.
16 Ibid., 57/17.
17 John A. Munro and Alex I. Inglis, eds, *Mike: The Memoirs of the Right Honourable Lester B. Pearson*, vol. 2: *1948–1957* (Toronto: University of Toronto Press and Signet, 1975), 308.
18 HC 26 November 1957, 1515.
19 Ibid., 23 January 1958, 3664.
20 Ibid.

21 Ibid., 24 January 1958, 3731–2.

CHAPTER FOUR

1 NA 10170-A-40.
2 DFPI 4, CV, 135, Eban to Sharett, 17 August 1949. In an earlier cable to Sharett, Eban noted that Canada was among those who did not favour "full freedom of arms purchases," in ibid., main vol.: 263.
3 NA 50,000-B-40 memorandum of 4 January 1950.
4 Ibid., 17 June, 18 October, and 10 November 1949.
5 ISA 2587/15/א, and 2598/9, Harman to Comay, 3 March 1950.
6 Ibid., 74/13/ב.
7 Ibid.
8 DFPI 5, 322.
9 NA 50,000-B-40, 5 January 1950.
10 Ibid., 9 January 1950.
11 PCO. It should be noted that at that time Defence Minister Brooke Claxton was acting EXA minister.
12 NA 50,000-B-40, 24 February 1950.
13 Ibid., 12 March 1950.
14 Ibid., and PCO vol. 20, 27 April 1950.
15 ISA 2587/15/א, Comay to Harman, 11 May 1950.
16 Ibid., Harman to Comay, 15 May 1950.
17 NA 50,00-B-40, 3 July 1950.
18 Ibid., and PCO vol. 21, 25 October 1950.
19 ISA 468/9, 8 May 1950.
20 ISA 2587-15-א, 19 April 1950.
21 Ibid., 31 May 1950. For a detailed account of Big Power involvement see Michael B. Oren, "Canada, the Great Powers, and the Middle Eastern Arms Race, 1950–56," *International History Review* 12, no. 2 (1990):260–300.
22 ISA 2587/15/א, 1 August 1950.
23 Ibid, 27 August 1950.
24 NA 50,00-B-40, 22 May 1951.
25 Ibid., 16 August 1951.
26 Ibid., 28 July 1952.
27 Ibid., 22 November 1952.
28 ISA 468/10, 20 and 21 August 1952.
29 Ibid., 20 and 27 August 1952.
30 Ibid., 27 August 1952.
31 NA 50,000-B-40, 5 September 1952.
32 Ibid., 5 January 1953.
33 ISA 2403/18/א, Nevo memorandum, 23 January 1953.

34 Ibid., 468/9, 17 February 1953.
35 Ibid.
36 NA 50,000-B-40, 4 March 1953.
37 ISA 468/9, 13 March 1953.
38 NA 50,000-B-40, 17 March 1953.
39 NA 50134–40, 18 June 1953.
40 Ibid.
41 Ibid.
42 NA 50,000-B-40, 13 July 1953.
43 HC 11 March 1953, 2832.
44 Ibid., 8 May 1953, 4978–9.
45 ISA 486/9.
46 NA 50,00-B-40, 4 September 1953.
47 ISA 2587/15/א, Comay to MABAR (British Commonwealth Division of Israeli Foreign Ministry), 14 September 1953.
48 Ibid.
49 NA 50,000-B-40, 11 September 1953.
50 Ibid., 22 September 1953.
51 ISA 2587/15/א, 12 October 1953.
52 Ibid.
53 NA 50,000-B-40, 9 October 1953.
54 ISA 2587/15/א, 8 October 1953.
55 Ibid., 18 October 1953.
56 NA 50,00-B-40, memoranda to minister, 16 and 22 October 1953.
57 Ibid., 19 October 1593.
58 Ibid., H.H. Wrong to minister, 26 November 1953.
59 Ibid., 16 December 1953.
60 ISA 2587/15/א, 23 December 1953.
61 NA 50,000-B-40, 5 January 1954.
62 ISA 2583/2, 13 January 1954.
63 Ibid.
64 NA 50,00-B-40, 27 January 1954.
65 Ibid., 9 february 1954.
66 ISA 2583/2, Comay minute of 14 March 1954.
67 Ibid., 2 March 1954.
68 John A. Munro and Alex I. Inglis, eds., *Mike: The Memoirs of the Right Honourable Lester B. Pearson*, vol. 2: *1948–1957* (Toronto: University of Toronto Press and Signet, 1975), 247–8.
69 NA 50,000-B-40, 12 and 28 April 1954.
70 Ibid., 9 June 1954.
71 Ibid., MacKay to minister, 30 June 954; Pearson to Comay, 8 July 1954. See also ISA 2587/15/א, for 6, 8, and 13 July 1954.
72 ISA 2587/15/א, 13 July 1954.

73 Such concern was also noted in a memorandum to Gershon Avner of the London Israeli embassy from Gideon Shomron of the Israeli Foreign Ministry in ibid., 10 August 1954.

74 NA 50,00-B-40, 7 July 1954.

75 Ibid., 17 September 1954.

76 Ibid., 8 and 9 September 1954.

77 Ibid., 18 October 1954.

78 Ibid., 18 and 21 October 1954.

79 Ibid., 10 December 1954.

80 Ibid., 13 January 1955.

81 Ibid.; see also of 13 January 1955.

82 Ibid., 21 January 1955.

83 Ibid., 25 March 1955.

84 ISA 2598/13, Ambassador MacDermott's visit in February–March 1955 to Israel, no date.

85 NA 50,000-B-40, 21 July 1955.

86 Ibid., 1 October 1955.

87 Ibid., 22 October and 7 November 1955.

88 Ibid., 30 November 1955.

89 Ibid.

90 ISA 2598/12, 29 September 1955.

91 Ibid., 25968/11, 29 November 1955. The appeal noted the close collaboration the two labour congresses and the HISTADRUT. See also Zachariah Kay, *Canada and Palestine: The Politics of Non-Commitment* (Jerusalem: Israel Universities Press, 1978), passim.

92 ISA 2598/14, 3 November 1955. The meeting is discussed in more detail in chapter 5.

93 Munro and Inglis, *Mike*, vol. 2, 249; also reported in detail in ISA 413/28 of 25 November 1955 and NA Pearson Papers, MG26 N1, vol. 37, 11 November 1955.

94 Munro and Inglis, *Mike*, vol. 2, 249.

95 Ibid., 251.

96 Discussed in greater detail in chapter 5.

97 ISA 2598/12, note of 5 December 1955.

98 NA 50,000-B-40, 2 December 1955.

99 ISA 2587/15/ב, 2 December 1955.

100 Ibid., 2598/5, Comay note of 27 December 1955; 413/28 of 27 December 1955.

CHAPTER FIVE

1 NA 50134–40, 13 April 1951.

2 Ibid., 9 November 1952.

3 Ibid., 23 November 1952.
4 Ibid., 21 November 1952.
5 Ibid., 24 November 1952. Note discussion on this matter in the General Assembly in chapter 2 above. On MacCallum and Pearson's early role see Anne Trowell Hilmer, "Here I am in the Middle: Lester Pearson and the Origins of Canada's Diplomatic Involvement in the Middle East," in David Taras and David Goldberg, *The Domestic Battleground* (Montreal: McGill-Queen's University Press, 1989), 125–43.
6 Confidential interview with a retired EXA official.
7 NA 50134–40, letters of 22 December 1952 and 18 January 1953.
8 See also EXA *Monthly Bulletin* 5, no. 2 (1953):57.
9 David Dewitt and John Kirton, *Canada as a Principal Power* (Toronto: John Wiley & Sons, 1983), 373.
10 ISA 2598/14, 8 February 1953.
11 Ibid.
12 ibid, 351/9, 26 October 1953.
13 Sir John Glubb Pasha, the British commander of the Hashemite Jordan's Arab Legion.
14 NA 50134–40, 10 November 1953.
15 Ibid.
16 ISA 2583/2, 13 April 1954.
17 Ibid, 2585/11, 13 April 1954.
18 NA 50134–40, 3 June 1954.
19 ISA 2598/12, 31 August 1954.
20 Ibid., 2583/2, 14 September 1954. See also chapter 4 above.
21 Ibid., 351/9 and 2585/11, 30 September 1954.
22 NA 50143–40, 20 October 1954, emphasis in original.
23 ISA 2583/2, 27 December 1954.
24 NA 50134–40, 29 December 1954.
25 Ibid.
26 ISA 2598/13, February–March 1955.
27 Ibid., no date.
28 ISA 2583/2, 31 March 1955.
29 John A. Munro and Alex I. Inglis, eds., *Mike: The Memoirs of the Right Honourable Lester B. Pearson*, vol. 2: *1948–1957* (Toronto: University of Toronto Press and Signet, 1975), 251.
30 Ibid., 252.
31 ISA 2583/2, 31 March 1955.
32 ISA 2598/7, 31 March 1955.
33 ISA 2583/2, 10 April 1955.
34 Ibid., 3 May 1955.
35 Ibid.

36 See E.L.M. Burns, *Between Arab and Israeli* (Toronto and Vancouver: Clarke Irwin, 1962), 71.

37 ISA 2598/12, 19 September 1955.

38 Ibid., 2598/14, 3 November 1955.

39 HC, 24 January 1956, 467.

40 ISA 2598/12, Comay's note of 5 December 1955.

41 Ibid.

42 Ibid., 2598/5, 27 December 1955; and NA Pearson Papers of 23 December 1955.

43 ISA 2598/5 and 413/28, 27 December 1955.

CHAPTER SIX

1 HC, 11 January 1956, 9.

2 Ibid., 17 January 1956, 184.

3 James Eayrs, *Canada in World Affairs, October 1955–June 1957* (Toronto: Oxford University Press, 1959), 247.

4 HC, 20 January 1956, 344–6; and 23 January 1956, 389.

5 Ibid., 462 et seq.

6 Ibid., 464.

7 Ibid.

8 Ibid., 465.

9 Ibid., 466.

10 Ibid.

11 Ibid., 468–9.

12 ISA 2598/5, Comay minute of 7 February 1956.

13 Ibid., 2598/14, 30 January 1956.

14 Ibid., Comay to McInnis of EXA, 31 January 1956.

15 HC, 6 February 1956, 880–1, 7 February, 911.

16 ISA 2598/14, 3 February 1956.

17 Ibid., Comay minute on 3 February meeting dated 7 February 1956.

18 Ibid., 13 February 1956.

19 HC, 7 February 1956, 942.

20 Ibid., 943–4.

21 Ibid., 15 and 17 February 1956, 1200, 1284.

22 Ibid., 6 March 1956, 1882–4.

23 Ibid., 6 March 1956, 1836.

24 Ibid., 8 March 1956, 1915–16.

25 Ibid., 9 March 1956, 1962–3.

26 Ibid., 16 March 1956, 2203–4.

27 S&S 56/9, 8.

28 Ibid., 9.

29 Ibid., 10.

30 ISA 2598/14. Eban to Jerusalem, 30 March 1956; and NA 50,000-B-40, Heeney to EXA, 29 March 1956.

31 NA 50,000-B-40, Heeney to EXA, 11 April 1956.

32 Ibid., 7 May 1956.

33 ISA 380/11, Comay minutes of 3 April 1956; and 2987/15/ב. See also NA 50,000-B-40, Minister to Ambassador in Washington, 3 April 1956.

34 ISA 2587/5/ב, 3 April 1956.

35 NA 50,000-B-40, 3 April 1956, and ISA 380/11, 3 April 1956.

36 ISA 380/11, 3 April 1956.

37 Ibid., 2598/13, S. Smilansky of MABAR to Israeli Embassy in London, 9 April 1956.

38 NA 50,000-B-40, 5 May 1956.

39 Ibid., record of date.

40 Ibid., 7 April 1956.

41 Ibid., 3 May 1956.

42 Ibid., Under-secretary to minister, 16 April 1956.

43 Ibid., 18 April 1956.

44 Minutes of proceedings and evidence, no. 2, 39.

45 Ibid., 41.

46 Ibid., 60.

47 ISA 2598/12, 30 April 1956. see also NA 50,000-B-40, 24 April 1956.

48 ISA 2598/12, 30 April 1956.

49 Ibid., 2598/13, 8 May 1956.

50 Ibid., 2597/15/ב, 24 and 27 April 1956.

51 Ibid., 25 April 1956.

52 NA 50,000-B-40, 30 April 1956.

53 Ibid., 19 May 1956.

54 NA 50360–40, 30 April 1956.

55 Ibid. (and memoranda of 23 and 24 April 1956).

56 Ibid., 30 April 1956.

57 Ibid., 21 May 1956.

58 Ibid.

59 NA 50,000-B-40, 10 May 1956. See also John A. Munro and Alex I. Inglis, eds., *Mike: The Memoirs of the Right Honourable Lester B. Pearson*, vol. 2: *1948–1957* (Toronto: University of Toronto Press and Signet, 1975), 252–4, as well as NA Pearson Papers of 10 May 1956.

60 NA 50,000-B-40, 10 May 1956.

61 Ibid., 14 May 1956.

62 ISA 2598/12, minute of 21 May 1956.

63 NA 50,000-B-40, record of meeting by A.E. Ritchie, 25 May 1956. Concern over the pipeline debate was communicated to MABAR by Comay in ISA 2598/11, 21 May and 7 June 1956.

64 NA 50,000-B-40, 23 May 1956.

65 Ibid., 24 May 1956.
66 ISA 2598/12, minute of 21 May 1956.
67 Ibid.
68 NA 50,000-B-40, 22 May 1956.
69 Ibid., and ISA 2598/12, 21 May 1956.
70 ISA 2598/12, 31 May and 4 June 1956.
71 Ibid., 1 June 1956 and NA Pearson Papers, 1 June 1956.
72 NA 50,000-B-40 and NA Pearson Papers, 1 June 1956.
73 NA 50,00-B-40, 8 June 1956.
74 Ibid., 11 June 1956.
75 Ibid., 13 June 1956.
76 NA 50360–40, 25 and 26 June 1956.
77 Ibid., 26 June 1956.
78 Ibid.
79 Ibid, Memorandum – Training of Israeli Service Personnel in Canada: Summary of 2 May 1958, 5.
80 NA 50,000-B-40, 14 June 1956.
81 ISA 2587/15/ג, Comay to MABAR, 12 June 1956.
82 Ibid., 18 June 1956.
83 Ibid., 328/1, 21 June 1956.
84 Ibid.
85 Ibid., 2598/12, 14 June 1956; NA 50,000-B-40, and NA 50360–40, 14 June 1956.
86 NA 50,000-B-40, 15 June 1956.
87 Ibid., 19 June 1956.
88 Ibid., Léger to Economic division re St Laurent meeting with Comay on 20 June 1956. The Léger memorandum contained a *Jerusalem Post* editorial of 15 June 1956 entitled "Promise and Performance." It described Canada as a good friend but resented U.S. prodding. It asked whether Canada was a butler and noted that the U.S. was attempting to act by proxy. The paper felt that those were high-handed American tactics *vis-à-vis* Canada.
89 NA 50,000-B-40 note of 21 June 1956, emphasis mine.
90 ISA 2583/2, 21 June 1956.
91 HC, 22 June 1956, 5322–3.
92 Ibid., 29 June 1956, 5517.
93 NA 50,000-B-40, 25 June 1956.
94 Ibid, 30 June 1956.
95 ISA 2598/12, 2 July 1956.
96 Ibid., Comay minute, 10 july 1956.
97 Ibid., 2583/2, two memoranda to MABAR, 10 July 1956.
98 HC, 9 July 1956, 5767.
99 Ibid., 11 July 1956, 5860–1.

100 Ibid., 5861.
101 Ibid, 5931.
102 NA Burns Papers, no date, but follows HC debates of 11 July 1956; Pearson message, emphasis mine.
103 NA 50,000-B-40, 11 July 1956. Professor Maxwell Cohen of the United Zionist Council proposed that the F-86s be sold unilaterally and be contingent on Israel's starting the proposed Jordan Water Diversion Project; in ibid., 12 July 1956.
104 Ibid, meeting of 13 July 1956, recorded by P. Campbell of EXA on 17 July 1956; and Comay minute, dated 16 July 1956 in ISA 2598/12.
105 ISA 2598/12, Schneerson of MABAR to Comay, 19 July 1956.
106 ISA 2587/15/ב, 13 July 1956.
107 HC, 20 July 1956, 6223.
108 Ibid., 6466.
109 NA 50,000-B-40, 25 and 27 July 1956.
110 Ibid., 27 July 1956.
111 Ibid., 26 July 1956, and NA Pearson Papers of same date.
112 Ibid., 27 July 1956 and ISA 2598/12, Comay minute of 30 July 1956.
113 ISA 2598/12, Comay minute of 30 July 1956.
114 Ibid., and chapter 7.
115 NA 50,000-B-40, 30 July 1956.
116 Ibid., 27 July 1956.
117 Ibid., 31 July 1956.
118 ISA 2587/16, Comay to MABAR, 3 August 1956.
119 Ibid., 2598/12, minute of 3 August 1956.
120 HC, 31 July 1956, 6717.
121 NA 50,000-B-40, minute of 14 August 1956 on cabinet meeting of 31 July 1956. In reply to many letters and telegrams it had received urging the shipment to Israel of the sabres, the government said, "There has been *no final refusal* on Canada's part to sell aircraft to Israel." Emphasis mine.
122 HC, 1 August 1956, 6793.
123 Ibid., 6800.
124 Ibid, 6808.
125 Ibid., 6827–9.
126 Ibid., 6831.
127 NA 50,000-B-40, 31 July and 3 August 1956; and ISA 2587/16, Comay to MABAR, 2 August 1956.
128 ISA 2587/16, Comay to MABAR, 2 and 5 August 1956.
129 NA 50,000-B-40, 7 and 9 August 1956.
130 Ibid., and ISA 2598/12, 23 August 1956.
131 NA 50,000-B-40, 21 August 1956.
132 Ibid., 24 August 1956 and Comay's *aide mémoire* of 25 August, which

noted that less than a squadron (twenty-four) would not be practical. See also ISA 2598/12 of 27 August 1956.

133 NA 50,000-B-40, Léger memorandum, 28 August 1956.

134 Ibid., 25 August 1956.

135 Ibid., Ford memorandum, 29 August 1956.

136 The total of twenty-four was subsequently approved; ibid., 29 August 1956.

137 NA 50,000-B-40, 31 August 1956, and ISA 2587/16, Comay cable to MABAR, 31 August 1956.

138 Dale C. Thomson, *Louis St Laurent: Canadian* (Toronto: Macmillan, 1967), 462.

139 NA 50,00-B-40, and NA Pearson Papers, 4 September 1956.

140 NA 50,000-B-40, 4 September 1956.

141 Ibid., Heeney to EXA, 6 September 1956.

142 Ibid., 10 September 1956.

143 Ibid., 12 September 1956.

144 Ibid., Martin to Pearson, 17 September 1956.

145 Ibid., Comay to Martin, 20 September 1956.

146 Ibid., 21 September 1956, and ISA 2587/16, 21 September 1956.

147 NA 50,000-B-40, 28 September 1956, and NA Pearson Papers, 28 September 1956.

148 NA 50,000-B-40, 28 September 1956 and ISA 2587/16, 21 September 1956.

149 NA 50,000-B-40.

150 Ibid., communications 5, 5 and 11 October 1956, and ISA 2587/16.

151 NA 50,000-B-40, 21 and 22 September 1956.

152 Ibid., letter to Pearson, 26 September 1956, and reply of 4 October 1956.

153 Ibid., A.E. Ritchie, memorandum, 3 October 1956.

154 Ibid., 26 September and 5 October 1956.

155 Ibid., 11 October 1956.

156 Ibid., 19 October 1956, and ISA 2587/16, 20 October 1956.

157 NA 50,000-B-40, 18 October 1956.

158 Ibid., 17 October 1956.

159 Ben Gurion Diaries, entry for 5 October 1956, in Ben Gurion Archives (hereafter BGA), Sdeh Boker, Israel.

160 ISA 2587/16, 15 October 1956.

161 John Holmes, *The Shaping of Peace: Canada and the Search for World Order*, vol. 2 (Toronto: University of Toronto Press, 1972, 356.

162 NA 50360–40, passim and especially despatches of late October.

163 See inter alia Prime Minister's address to the nation, 4 November 1956, S&S 56/24; and Fourth Special session, 22nd parliament, 26 November 1956.

164 NA 50,000-B-40, McInnis to under-secretary, 30 October 1956. Pearson later told parliament in reply to Diefenbaker's query that the prime minister's statement of 31 October 1956, "did not express judgment on the Israeli action in Egypt." HC, 7 February 1957, 1048.

165 HC, 7 February 1957, 1048.

166 NA 50,000-B-40, 31 October 1956.

167 Ibid., 5 November 1956.

168 Ibid., and ISA 2598/12 of 5 and 6 November 1956.

169 NA 50,000-B-40, 7 November 1956.

170 Ibid., 8 November 1956.

171 ISA 3122/11, 30 and 31 December 1956 and NA 50,000-B-40, 27 and 31 December 1956.

172 NA 50,000-B-40, 9 January 1957.

173 HC, 6 February 1957, 1011–12, Howe response to Diefenbaker.

174 Ibid.

175 David Ben-Gurion, *"Ben-Gurion Looks Back" in Talks with Moshe Pearlman* (London: Weidenfeld and Nicholson, 1965), 168.

176 ISA 3122/16, Lourie to Comay, 29 November 1957.

177 Holmes, *The Shaping of Peace*, vol. 2, 381.

CHAPTER SEVEN

1 Ilan Troen as quoted in Z. Kay, "Public opinion played part in Suez debacle," *Winnipeg Free Press*, 21 November 1986.

2 Z. Kay, "Thirty years later, Suez crisis seen as Europe's Waterloo," *Winnipeg Free Press*, 20 November 1986.

3 Ibid.

4 Fuller details can be found in Z. Kay, "The UN Forces in Korea and Sinai: Some thoughts in retrospect," *International Relations* 2, no. 3 (1961): 168–83; and Graham Spry, "Canada, the United Nations Emergency Force and the Commonwealth," *International Affairs* 33, no. 3 (1957).

5 S&S 56/24, 4 November 1956, 2.

6 EXA, *Monthly Bulletin* 8, no. 12 (1956):362.

7 HC Special session, 26 November 1956, 5 et seq.

8 Kay, "UN Forces" 174–5; and James Eayrs, *Canada in World Affairs, October 1955–June 1957* (Toronto: Oxford University Press, 1959), 267–71.

9 HC, 26 November 1956, 29.

10 Canada, Senate Debates, 29 November 1956, 36–41.

1 ISA 3122/5, Lorne Ingle, National secretary of the CCF to MAPAI, 4 December 1956.

12 ISA 3128/18, Moshe Erell's report on the convention, 17 December 1956.

13 ISA 3122/11, Comay to Pearson, 15 and 19 December 1956.

14 Ibid., 3122/20, discussed between Canadian embassy first secretary Maybee and Israel's Shimon Arad, 20 December 1956.

15 Ibid., 3122/11, Comay minute on the St Laurent-Meir talks, 17 December 1956.

16 HC, 9 January 1957, 29.

17 Ibid., 178–9.

18 Ibid., 179.

19 Ibid., 178.

20 Ibid., 176.

21 ISA 328/1, 17 January 1957.

22 S&S 57/7.

23 ISA 328/1, 27 January 1957; 3122/14, 26 January 1957; discussion included Eban.

24 S&S 57/9, 27 January 1957, 3, emphasis mine.

25 United Nations document A/3512. See also Kay, "UN Forces," 176–8.

26 S&S 57/11, 2 February 1957.

27 Kay, "UN Forces," 177–8.

28 HC, 17 January 1957, 353.

29 Ibid., 21 January 1957, 455.

30 Ibid., 25 January 1957, 639.

31 Ibid., 640.

32 Ibid., 30 January 1957, 801–2.

33 Ibid., 809.

34 Ibid., 810.

35 Ibid., 816.

36 Ibid., 817.

37 Ibid., 820.

38 Ibid., 1 February 1957, 877–9.

39 Ibid., 7 February 1957, 1047.

40 Ibid., 1048.

41 ISA 3122/14, 11 February 1957.

42 Ibid., 3122/20, 12 February 1957.

43 Ibid.

44 HC, 19 February 1957, 1415.

45 Ibid., 21 February 1957, 1503.

46 S&S 57/17, 8.

47 Ibid., 9.

48 HC, 26 February 1957, 1650.

49 Kay, "UN Forces," 179.

50 Leopold Yehuda Laufer, "The perils of the 'Schnorrer' Mentality," *Jerusalem Post*, 5 November 1990.

51 HC, 15 March 1957, 2354.

52 s&s 57/20, 4.
53 ISA 3050/14, 6 March 1957.
54 Confidential interview with one who was deeply involved in the matter.
55 HC, 11 March 1957, 2060–1.
56 Ibid., 2061–2.
57 Ibid., 12 March 1957, 2109–11.
58 Ibid., 14 March 1957, 2186.
59 Ibid., 15 March 1957, 2352.
60 Ibid., 2352–3.
61 Ibid., 2353.
62 Ibid.
63 Ibid., 2356.
64 Ibid., 2357.
65 Ibid., 2359.
66 Ibid., 2360.
67 Ibid., 2362.
68 Ibid., 2363.
69 Ibid., 2366.
70 ibid., 2369.
71 Ibid., 2369–70.
72 Ibid., 2371.
73 Ibid., 2372.
74 Ibid., 2374.
75 Ibid., 2375.
76 Ibid., 2376.
77 Ibid., 2378 see also Zachariah Kay, *Canada and Palestine: The Politics of Non-Commitment* (Jerusalem: Israel Universities Press, 1978).
78 HC, 15 March 1957, 2377–9.
79 Ibid., 2386.
80 Ibid., 2387.
81 Ibid., 2388–9.
82 Ibid., 2394.
83 ISA 3122/20, 16 March 1957.
84 NA 50,000-B-40, 15 March 1957.
85 ISA 328/1, 18 March 1957.
86 HC, 18 March 1957, 2400.
87 Ibid.
88 Ibid., 19 March 1957, 2453; see also 21 March 1957, 2543.
89 Ibid., 22 March 1957, 2589.
90 Ibid., 2589–90.
91 ISA 3122/14, 27 March 1957.
92 HC, 27 March 1957, 2736.
93 ISA 328/1, 1 April 1957.

94 s&s 57/26, "The Present Position of the United Nations," address to the Women's Canadian Club, Saint John, NB, 4 April 1957, 6.

95 Ibid., 57/27, "The United Nations, the Middle East and Canadian Foreign Policy," address to a joint meeting of the Men's and Women's Canadian Clubs, Halifax, NS, 5 April 1957, 7.

96 Ibid., 57/25, "Searching for Peace in Palestine," address on the occasion of the Negev Dinner by the Montreal Jewish community honouring L.D. Crestohl, MP, Monday, 8 April 1957, 7.

97 Ibid., 9.

98 HC, 10 April 1957, 3360–1.

99 Ibid., 12 April 1957, 3491–2.

100 Canada, Senate Debates, 3 April 1957, 472–3.

101 NA 50,000-B-40, 15 March 1957, and 12 April 1957.

102 ISA 3122/11, 10 April 1957, re the meeting with Comay of 8 April 1957.

103 Ibid.

104 Ibid., 19 April 1957.

105 BGA, Comay of Canada: diary entry of 13 April 1957.

106 ISA 3122/11, 6 May 1957.

107 Ibid., 3122/25, 6 and 8 May 1957, including written communication to Pearson from M. Garber, president of the United Zionist Council of Canada and S. Bronfman, president of the Canadian Jewish Congress.

108 Ibid., 9 May 1957.

109 NA 50,00-B-40, 5 September 1957, and 50360–70, vol. 1

110 ISA 3122/20, 15 August 1957.

111 EXA Monthly Bulletin 9, no. 10 (1957).

112 HC, 14 October 1957, 123; and 21 October, 179–80.

113 Ibid., 19 November 1957, 1279–80.

114 Ibid., 1280.

115 Ibid., 26 November 1957, 1506.

116 David B. Dewitt and John Kirton, Canada as a Principal Power: A Study in Foreign Policy and International Relations (Toronto: John Wiley and Sons, 1983), 377.

117 HC, 26 November 1957, 1515.

118 See discussion in chapter 3.

119 ISA 3122/25, 10 December 1957.

120 John Holmes, The Shaping of Peace: Canada and the Search for World Order, vol. 2 (Toronto: University of Toronto Press, 1972), 349.

Index